# VIETNAM NOW

*A Case for Normalizing Relations with Hanoi*

## John LeBoutillier

Introduction by Richard M. Nixon
Foreword by Liz Trotta

PRAEGER

New York
Westport, Connecticut
London

**Library of Congress Cataloging-in-Publication Data**

LeBoutillier, John.
    Vietnam now : a case for normalizing relations
with Hanoi / John LeBoutillier.
        p.    cm.
    Bibliography:    p.
    Includes index.
    ISBN 0–275–93278–8 (alk. paper)
    1. United States—Foreign relations—Vietnam.    2. Vietnam—Foreign
relations—United States    I. Title.
E183.8.V5L43        1989
327.730597—dc19                89–3670

Library of Congress Catalog Card Number: 89–3670
ISBN: 0–275–93278–8

First published in 1989

Praeger Publishers, One Madison Avenue, New York, NY 10010
A division of Greenwood Press, Inc.

Printed in the United States of America

The paper used in this book complies with the Permanent
Paper Standard issued by the National Information Standards
Organization (Z39.48–1984).

10 9 8 7 6 5 4 3 2 1

*To the hundreds of American Prisoners of War, still held against their will, who will be freed only when there is a new relationship between Washington and Hanoi.*

# CONTENTS

# INTRODUCTION

It is easy for Americans to say that today's communist rulers in Vietnam have gotten just what they bargained for: the status of an impoverished Soviet client state. During the Vietnam War, Hanoi's propaganda, and its witting and unwitting propagandists in the West, claimed it was waging a "war of national liberation" against the U.S.-backed South Vietnamese. The claim is particularly ironic in view of the way the war ended, with Saigon totally independent and bereft of U.S. support and Hanoi totally in hock to the Soviet Union.

Under the terms of the Paris Peace Accords of 1973, the United States was permitted to give Saigon the same amount of support as the Soviet Union provided Hanoi. Within two years the Congress had slashed aid to almost nothing, while Moscow massively increased its aid. North Vietnamese commanders noted with satisfaction that the Americans were forcing their friends to fight a "poor man's war." Even so, in almost two years South Vietnam did not lose a single provincial capital to the North, whose final victory in April 1975 would have been inconceivable without Moscow's support—and Washington's abandonment of Saigon.

After 1975, Vietnam learned what it costs to accept Moscow's largesse. The Soviets, eager for bases to counter the U.S. presence in the Philippines, moved into Cam Ranh Bay and Danang and stationed thousands of soldiers and other military personnel in the country. They sent the Vietnamese army into Cambodia, a move that served Soviet interests by threatening China, allies of Cambodia's Khmer Rouge rulers. They shipped Vietnamese workers to Siberia and absorbed whatever agricultural surpluses Vietnam's crippled Stalinist economy could produce.

Today, Vietnam is one of the poorest nations in the world. Twenty years ago, despite the rigors of war, South Vietnam managed to export rice; today communist Vietnam cannot feed its own people. As they take their first halting steps toward economic reform, Vietnam's leaders are realizing that Moscow has nothing more to offer, while the West has everything to offer. The question is: What does Vietnam have to offer us? What does the United States have to gain from a normalization of relations with Vietnam?

In the years since he left Congress, John LeBoutillier has dedicated countless hours to trying to learn the fate of Americans who are still missing in action in Vietnam. The conclusions he reaches in *Vietnam Now: A Case for Normalizing Relations with Hanoi* grow partially from his passionate beliefs that Americans remain alive in Southeast Asia and that Hanoi will assist in locating them as part of a normalization deal. He also makes a persuasive case for other strategic and humanitarian benefits that might result if the United States and Vietnam established diplomatic and other relations.

LeBoutillier believes the choice is ours. I believe it is theirs. Vietnam must choose whether it wants the benefits of a better relationship with the United States or the grinding burden of continuing to provide a base for Soviet ambitions in Indochina and the Pacific. It must make its choice clear before any U.S. President should consider normalizing relations. The United States must never be in the position of subsidizing a Soviet outpost, in Vietnam, Cuba, or anywhere else.

There are encouraging signs that the Vietnamese occupation of Cambodia will end by 1990. I would not be surprised if Mikhail Gorbachev, as part of his global PR offensive and military belt tightening, announced a withdrawal of Soviet forces stationed at Cam Ranh Bay. These would be two important signposts on the road to better relations between our two countries.

But a decoupling of Soviet and Vietnamese interests is not enough. While I do not share the author's optimism that Americans are still alive in Indochina, I do share his conviction that all Americans must be accounted for. Hanoi must satisfactorily answer all outstanding inquiries on the POWs and MIAs before we should move toward normalization. As the president who presented too many Medals of Honor to the grieving families of victims of Hanoi's aggression and welcomed home too many victims of torture and neglect in its POW camps, I could not support a policy that rewards Hanoi before the fact. If Vietnam knows where prisoners are, let us see them. If Vietnam still has remains of Americans who died for their country, let their families have them. A cold calculation of U.S. security interests rather than an accounting of the MIAs should be the motive behind any move toward normalization. But normalization is unthinkable without such an accounting.

I admire John LeBoutillier's impassioned dedication to the MIA issue. I recommend his book to any American who wants to understand today's Vietnam and the strategic issues at stake in southeast Asia. We disagree about timing and tactics. But we agree on the important thing: Vietnam should someday be free. That is why I pursued the policies I did in the Vietnam War. That is why I hope that someday soon Vietnam will earn the right to be welcomed into the family of civilized nations.

*Richard M. Nixon*

# FOREWORD

In 1973, as a member of the first "official" press contingent allowed into North Vietnam, I stood in the dusty courtyard of the stern prison camp known as the "Hanoi Hilton," awaiting the release of American prisoners. After years of covering the struggle in Vietnam, my colleagues and I were getting our first close-up of the enemy, and in their very heartland. More important, within days we would hear tales of brutality that confirmed our darkest fears. Who could forget those haggard, ill-clad men shuffling down the airplane ramp. Or the blurred black and white photos of skeletal figures slumped in solitary confinement. More than any one impression, America's POWs were the supreme image of its national agony.

With the airmen's release under the Paris accords, one chapter closed. For most journalists, their role as chroniclers was over, essentially if not actually, not just as professionals, but as witnesses to an event that had pulverized our hometowns, our friendships, and our families, even our self-esteem. Frankly, it was a relief to get out and reassigned, to be alive and ready to reap the benefits of having stuck with a tough assignment. Newspapers, magazines, wire services, and networks cut back or closed their Southeast Asia bureaus. Editors and executive producers turned their attention and their correspondents elsewhere. Vietnam was retreating into the crumbling files of old news.

If the 1960s assaulted us with a tireless, self-righteous drumming on the "immorality" of what Noam Chomsky was to a call "war with Asia," and on the wickednesses, blindnesses, and failures of the preceding generation, then the silence of the postwithdrawal period was even more deafening; that is, until Saigon fell in 1975, with the subsequent mass flight of the boat people from their "liberators," and the holocaust of millions that Pol Pot offered up to marxism in Cambodia. Then an enlightened Hollywood discovered the possibilities of jungle war and with it the not always delicate simplicities of *Rambo* and *Platoon*. Nor must we forget the professionally poignant tellers of war stories weeping for the evening news at the memorial wall in Washington. Vietnam never did inspire moderation. And, true to form, its awakened memories sifted back to reinflame the national consciousness. The trouble was, and is, that talking about the war so often provides an excuse to refight it.

On the day in 1940 when Hitler's Luftwaffe began its bombardment of Britain, Sir Winston Churchill addressed the House of Commons: "If we open a quarrel between the past and the present, we shall find that we have lost the future." He wanted to get on with it. And so might we. That is why the thesis of this book— that the United States should establish normal relations with the Hanoi government—is a timely if not modest proposal for this age of the Pacific Rim, an era of foreign policy in which economic considerations are eclipsing military ones, in which past bitterness and humiliation can be offset by civilized interchange.

That the suggestion of seeking a closer rapprochement with a still-triumphant, doctrinaire communist regime should come from a known conservative is striking. One wonders why the very people who forged an impassioned alliance with our enemy during the war years seem to have drifted away. A few have recanted. Most have simply told their stories of romantic Cong exploits and moved on to Central America. Where are they now—perhaps just when we at last need them.

In this provocative book, John LeBoutillier raises a second point that, if now answered, will haunt us forever—the possibility that not every American prisoner was set free, that even now some may still be alive and in prison. Such ghostly possibilities have haunted the aftermath of many wars. Often they are lumped with theories about the Kennedy assassination or about what really happened to Jimmy Hoffa. Many people simply mutter "crackpot." Yet in the absence of hard information to the contrary, it seems fair and reasonable to call for an open reexamination of the considerable number of cases of American servicemen known to have been at some point alive during captivity, but who, nevertheless, were not repatriated in 1973.

To wake up one day and discover that we have "lost the future" to old resentments or diplomatic bungling would be to miss the trenchant lessons of our experience in Southeast Asia. Let us hope the next time we see an American helicopter lifting off from a rooftop in Saigon, it will be carrying tourists, instead of refugees.

*Liz Trotta*

# PREFACE

The United States of America should immediately change its policy toward Vietnam. With no preconditions whatsoever, the United States should normalize relations with the regime in Hanoi. Ambassadors should be exchanged; embassies should be set up.

Following this first step of diplomatic recognition, Washington should announce a schedule of other bilateral relationships with Vietnam; for example, lift the trade embargo, discuss granting most favored nation trading status, and help secure loans from the World Bank, the International Monetary Fund, and the Asian Development Bank. All of these steps should only be taken in conjunction with reciprocal steps taken on outstanding bilateral issues by Hanoi; for instance, settle the vexing POW/MIA issue, release all Amerasian children, release political prisoners, and withdraw from Kampuchea. Furthermore, the United States should increase economic and military aid to the non-Communist resistance in Kampuchea and increase military assistance to Thailand. These two changes will send a clear signal to Hanoi: the United States, in attempting to establish a more friendly relationship with Hanoi, will not tolerate Vietnamese aggression against Thailand, our ally, and will not accept an illegal invasion of Kampuchea, a sovereign state.

The present U.S. policy toward Vietnam is simplistic: There will be no relations whatsoever until Hanoi removes its forces from Kampuchea and allows the Kampuchean people to select their own government. In addition, there will be no relations whatsoever until

a full accounting is made of all the missing Americans from the
Vietnam War.

The argument of this book is that present U.S. policy is so
fundamentally flawed and inconsistent that it has directly contributed to greatly increased Soviet influence in Southeast Asia. This
policy has isolated Vietnam and forced the Vietnamese into the
Soviet orbit. Thus, Moscow has obtained an invaluable toehold in
the world's most rapidly growing region. Furthermore, what has
been accomplished? Vietnam, we see, is still occupying Kampuchea. On the emotionally charged POW/MIA issue, we see almost
no progress. The thousands of Amerasian children remaining in
Vietnam continue to haunt us. The release of Vietnamese political
prisoners, many of whom worked for the United States during the
war, continues to be put off. Clearly, this current policy does not
serve any U.S. interest.

Thirteen years after the last American helicopter took off from
the U.S. embassy in Saigon, it is not popular to argue that we
should attempt a new relationship with Vietnam. Few books and
only a handful of articles point in such a direction. Of course, in
the mid-1960s, few Americans were prepared to challenge U.S.
policy toward Vietnam either. Only with the deaths of thousands
of troops did the people and government of the United States enter
a debate about our policy in Vietnam.

Now, in the late 1980s, with no American soldiers being sent to
Vietnam, it is easy to ignore and forget that region of the world.
In doing so, we dishonor those who fought and those who died.
Moreover, we endanger our allies and ourselves.

This book sets forth a plan to reverse course in Southeast Asia.
It is based in part on the belief that the United States is threatened
not by Vietnam, but by the Soviet Union, specifically by a new
Soviet strategy in the Pacific. The plan proposed here is rooted in
the belief that the United States needs to learn how to act as a
superpower and to use the lessons of the past to set present policy.
The United States of America is the world's only true superpower—
a dominant power both militarily and economically. This combination of military and economic strength, when exercised correctly,
transforms into unquestioned diplomatic power.

This country's problem in Southeast Asia comes from a fundamental misunderstanding of U.S. power by national leaders. The

United States has played the shrinking violet and has thus abdicated a leadership role in the region. Moscow has entered this vacuum, using both Vietnam and Kampuchea as cornerstones of its Pacific strategy.

This book argues that Vietnam, under new leadership, is now ready to become independent of Moscow. The Hanoi regime, which fought for decades for independence from the French and then from the Americans, did not do so to become a client of the Soviets.

The United States should now reassert itself in Southeast Asia. First, normalize relations with Vietnam. One immediate result will be competition in the region between the Americans, the Soviets, and the Chinese. The United States and its free-enterprise allies will win this competition.

# ACKNOWLEDGMENTS

Special thanks go to Cassie Winsett, Elsie Hillman, Jimmy Walker, Mrs. Elaine Moseley, Mrs. A. C. Bostwick, Jamie Humes, Bill Timmons, John Taylor, John Thornton, Anthony D. Duke, John M. G. Brown, Jeff B. Ledbetter, Barry Gray, William Simon, Charlton Heston, Bill Caplan, Jeremiah Milbank, George Champion, Jim Pinkerton, Walter Curley, Roger Ailes, Jane Eberle, Ron Miller, Nguyen Dang Quang, Tony Cicatiello, Ed Derwinski, Tom Kean, Marylou Whitney, Helen Muller, John Cardinal O'Connor, Barbara Newington, Judge Eddie Sapir, Barbara Keenan, and Mary Matejov.

I would also like to thank my two excellent research assistants: Kathleen McEvoy and Hugh Mansfield.

This book would not exist without the excellent editing of Jack McVey and the corrections and alterations suggested by Janet Drohan, my wonderful secretary.

Most of all, thanks to Frank Ashburn for years of support, thanks to my brother Tim Secor for exhibiting tremendous courage through an extremely difficult personal tragedy, and thanks to my mother for her lifetime of love and help to all her children.

# VIETNAM NOW

# 1

# AMERICA RETURNS TO VIETNAM

## I

Before the early 1990s end, the United States of America could bring military forces back to Vietnam, back to the U.S.-built bases at Cam Ranh Bay and Danang. Only this time, the U.S. ships, planes, and soldiers would not be uninvited combatants, but instead would be guests of the new Vietnamese government in Hanoi.

In a stunning policy reversal, the newly installed reformist regime in Vietnam wants to move out of its almost total dependency on Moscow and toward a more open, friendly relationship with the United States. As a part of that new move, Hanoi's leaders are offering Washington the opportunity to alter the strategic military balance in the Pacific. At a time when the Soviets are expanding their reach throughout Southeast Asia and the Philippine government has threatened not to renew the leases for the two U.S. bases in the Philippines, Subic Bay, and Clark Field, Hanoi is offering a new alternative: a lease agreement for the United States to use the bases it originally built in Vietnam over twenty-five years ago.

This amazing Vietnamese offer was matter-of-factly presented to me by two high-level Vietnamese foreign ministry officials as we drove outside Hanoi in the back seat of a Soviet Volga limousine. I had been invited to Vietnam by the Hanoi government to discuss how to improve relations between the two nations. Before and during my trip, the many government officials I met told me of their frustration in dealing with the Reagan administration. It seemed that no one from Washington would even listen to offers from the Vietnamese. The only official in the Reagan administration assigned to talk to the Vietnamese was an army lieutenant colonel on the staff of the National Security Council. Hanoi considered him to be a political lightweight.

I was sandwiched between the two men in the back of the car as we returned from a day-long visit to the famed Perfume Pagoda, forty miles southeast of Hanoi. Our driver, Ha, could put Mario Andretti to shame. Vietnamese streets are constantly crowded with bicycles. Cars have to weave in and out of this almost-tidal wave of bikes. Ha, always sporting a stylish blue beret and a denim leisure suit, needed three hands: one for the steering wheel, one for the stick shift, and another for the horn. That is what you first notice in Vietnam: the drivers lean on that horn continually, warning bikers to move out of the way. The people on the bicycles only begrudgingly respond, split microseconds before being run over by the car. They slide to the side of the road, allowing the car to pass, a look of resentment in their eyes.

Politically, I soon began to wonder if this nearly open animosity between auto and bike didn't best illustrate the Soviet-Vietnamese problem: almost every motor car in Hanoi belongs to a Soviet or Eastern bloc diplomat. Even high-level Vietnamese government officials are too poor to have a car; they, too, ride bikes to work. Thus, if you are a Vietnamese on your bike and a car approaches from behind with its horn blaring in your ears, the odds are it belongs to a Soviet. It is no secret today in Vietnam that the Soviets, who are seen as boorish and clumsily arrogant, have worn out their welcome.

Amid the horn tooting and the wave of bikes, I casually asked my two Vietnamese escorts, "Do you think the day could ever come when the United States military could have access to Vietnamese military facilities?" I was gently probing. Without hesitation, both officials responded with identical statements: "The day after the United States normalizes relations with Vietnam, we are prepared to open negotiations with Washington to work out an agreement whereby America can have access to Cam Ranh Bay and Danang."

In Vietnam, officials of this level of the foreign ministry never make policy statements unless they have been authorized to do so by their superiors. They are almost robotlike in making statements and in asking questions designed to solicit information. So when two of them made this identical statement, it was obvious to me that it had come from above. I probed further, only to learn that, indeed, this is a genuine new offer from the recently installed government in Hanoi. It is an offer that could entirely restructure the superpower balance throughout the Pacific.

Perhaps most surprising about this startling new development is that no one from Washington had ever even bothered to ask Vietnam's leaders about the possibility of the United States returning to the two bases. Why not? Because there are not normalized relations between the United States and Vietnam; there is no regular dialogue. The only talking between these two former adversaries, infrequent and irregular as it is, concerns matters left over from the war: missing American soldiers, Amerasian children, the release of political prisoners, and the Vietnamese invasion of Kampuchea (Cambodia).

Except to consider these issues, none of them of vital U.S. strategic importance, Washington has deliberately chosen to hide its head in the sand and relive the war, wrapped up in a combination of guilt, spite, and bitterness.

Meanwhile, Moscow has circled like a vulture and swooped down on Vietnam, picking it dry and using the remains for its own strategic design: to become the major player throughout the Pacific.

Sadly, Washington's failure to act has allowed Moscow to expand its reach. The United States' mistaken policy since the end of the war in 1975 has driven Hanoi into a position of almost total dependency upon Moscow. In the process, Vietnam's economy and infrastructure have drastically deteriorated. As a result, Hanoi has removed its hard-line pro-Soviet government and replaced it with a group of pragmatic reformists who are willing to experiment with free-enterprise innovations. To this new regime's potentially historic offer to allow the United States to come back and use the bases in Vietnam, Washington has turned a deaf ear.

## II

Not long after founding the Soviet Union, Vladimir Lenin prescribed the Soviet gameplan for the Pacific: "Let us turn our faces toward Asia. The East will help us conquer the West." Years later, Joseph Stalin echoed this view in studying the lessons of the Second World War: "Victory in Europe might be won first in Asia."

Indeed, as the last U.S. helicopter took off from the roof of the U.S. embassy in Saigon in late April 1975, Moscow's military planners were already preparing to exploit the inevitable vacuum. Hanoi, exhausted after years of combat, had few allies. China, to the north, had at best a difficult relationship with Hanoi. The United States had no intention of helping to rebuild the shattered economy and infrastructure of Vietnam, as it had done in Japan and Germany after World War II. Thus, Hanoi's victorious leaders were forced to rely on Moscow for economic and military assistance.

The Soviets, however, saw Vietnam as the central ingredient in their new aggressive Pacific strategy. Moscow's plan was to become the dominant player throughout the Pacific, from Nicaragua's western coast to Vladivostok. Vital to this plan was securing rights to the two former U.S. bases at Cam Ranh Bay and Danang. Thus, Moscow's price for economic and military aid to Vietnam was access to these facilities. Hanoi's leaders had little choice but to relent. Soon began a huge Soviet influx of military equipment, planes, submarines, dry docks, technical advisers, radar installations, and intelligence gathering equipment.

Along with this military buildup, strictly for Soviet purposes, came some second-tier Soviet economic aid for Vietnam. In the late 1970s, when Vietnam began to experience chronic food shortages, Moscow provided Hanoi with rice, foodstuffs, fertilizer, and other crude agricultural necessities, but as the Soviet economy itself began to deteriorate, the quality and amount of Soviet aid to Vietnam also declined.

The Vietnamese were in no position to complain. After generations of successfully fighting against outside dominance, they had forced themselves to be reliant once again upon an outside power: the Soviet Union. But, unlike the French and the Americans, both of whom possessed healthy, growing economies, the Soviets themselves were a failing economic power and had little to offer Vietnam. Soviet energy was devoted to building military capability in Southeast Asia.

## III

Today, as Admiral James Lyons said in a visit to Sydney, Australia, the Soviet presence in Vietnam is startling. The two bases at Cam Ranh Bay and Danang are "the site of the largest concentration of Soviet naval units and aircraft deployed to a naval facility outside the Warsaw Pact." Cam Ranh Bay has become the site of the largest naval forward deployment base outside the USSR.

This is especially significant when contrasted to the Soviet military position in the Pacific and especially Southeast Asia twenty years ago. As two noted Soviet experts have explained in *Soviet Policy*, "In the early 1960's, the Soviet Union lacked an ocean-going navy, sea-based air power, long-range transport aircraft and amphibian shipping. She could not maintain a fleet at sea and had few friendly ports of call. Even her merchant marine was small and lacked the kind of heavy lift equipment needed to off-load items like tanks in countries with minimal dockyard facilities. She had no special roll-on/roll-off shipping for the rapid disembarkation of vehicles. By the end of the 1970s, all but one of these disadvantages, the lack of sea-based airpower, had been remedied."

Cam Ranh Bay is the gemstone of the Soviet Pacific buildup. The Soviet Pacific navy has now become the largest of its four fleets. It is no coincidence that the Pacific is the primary area of growth for the Soviet navy. The architect of its modern navy, the late Admiral Segei G. Gorshkov, was quoted in *The Sea Power of the Soviet State* as saying, "The constantly growing maritime might of our country ensures our ability to enlarge our exploitation of the colossal natural resources of the World Ocean. The growing might of our country ensures the successful implementation of her foreign policy and allows us to widen our trading, shipping, scientific, and cultural links with other countries. Naval power has always been one of the historical factors determining the transformation of states into great powers."

With this in mind, Moscow eagerly moved to fill the vacuum after the U.S. evacuation in 1975. Once the Soviets got their hands on Cam Ranh Bay and Danang, they quickly built their new aggressive Pacific strategy around these two prizes. At any time at Cam Ranh Bay, over 30 Soviet naval vessels are based there, including surface combat ships, submarines, and a large floating dry dock. Recently, the Soviets completed work on a seventh pier, which increased dock space by 20 percent. Besides the naval base itself, the Soviets have also built at Cam Ranh Bay a composite air unit and a growing communications system, intelligence collection, and logistics support infrastructure. They have also based at least 8 TU-95 strategic bombers and 16 of their 240 Badger (YU-16) medium-range fighter bombers. Thousands of Soviet support personnel are stationed there, as well. One noted military affairs expert Brendan Greeley in *Aviation Week* in 1987, called this Soviet airpower buildup "the only Russian strike aircraft deployed anywhere in the world beyond Soviet borders." This is indicative not only of the importance Moscow places on these two bases, but also on the security the Soviets feel in their relationship with Hanoi.

However, as insurance against the possibility of a change for the worse in Moscow-Hanoi relations, the Soviets have used their multi- billion-dollar military support program for Vietnam to guarantee a lasting military presence in the region. After financing and encouraging the Vietnamese invasion of Kampuchea in late 1978, the Soviets themselves moved into Kampuchea. They quickly acquired the already existing naval facility at Kompong Son and spent heavily to rebuild and refurbish it. Moscow then began construction of an entirely new deep-water naval base at Ream.

With these two entirely Soviet facilities in Kampuchea, the Soviets have become masters of their own destiny in Southeast Asia.

Certainly the Soviet presence in Vietnam and Kampuchea is not for the protection of Hanoi nor is it defensive in nature. Indeed, General Secretary Mikhail Gorbachev clearly intends to use the increased Soviet encampment in the scope of superpower politics. In 1986, the Soviet leader said in a speech, "In general I would like to say that if the United States gave up its military presence, say, in the Philippines, we would not leave this step unanswered." Obviously, the United States will not voluntarily surrender Subic Bay and Clark Field. This Soviet offer indicates Moscow's grand design: to reduce the U.S. presence in Asia, leading to a position of superiority in the region for Moscow.

Indeed, Gorbachev announced his new Pacific strategy by saying in Vladivostok, "The Soviet Union is . . . an Asian and Pacific country." What goes on in the region "is for us a national, state interest." And Vietnam—with its two bases—plays a crucial role in this strategy. Moscow's tactics concerning Southeast Asia appear to be (1) to dominate the region ideologically, without having to win such dominance through war; (2) to prevent Japan from moving more heavily into the region; (3) to prevent a resurgent U.S. presence in Southeast Asia; (4) to contain and neutralize China, isolating Beijing militarily and diplomatically; and (5) to seduce the member states of the Association of Southeast Asian Nations (ASEAN), bringing them closer to the Soviet orbit.

The bases in Vietnam and Kampuchea allow Moscow to exert military muscle, but it is through massive amounts of economic assistance that the Soviet Union had been able to keep Hanoi locked firmly in Moscow's grip. Beginning shortly before the late 1978 Soviet-encouraged invasion of Kampuchea, the Vietnamese and Soviets signed the Friendship and Cooperation Treaty. Under the terms of this treaty, Moscow was to provide between $1 billion and $2 billion annually in economic aid. Added to this investment, the Soviets have provided Vietnam with 97 percent of their military equipment. In total, it is estimated that Hanoi receives between $3 million and $6 million per day from Moscow. Furthermore, in order to keep Vietnam even more dependent on the Soviet Union, beginning in 1984 Moscow considered everything given to Hanoi to be in the form of long-term loans, thereby requiring repayment. Prior aid had been in the form of grants and gifts.

More evidence of the almost-total Vietnamese dependence upon the Soviets is seen in the percentages of imports Hanoi receives from Moscow. For example, 90 percent of petroleum, 77 percent of food imports, 95 percent of cotton imports, and 90 percent of steel and chemical fertilizer come from the Soviet Union.

Recent reports indicate that, because of the rapidly disintegrating Vietnamese economy and continued Vietnamese diplomatic isolation, Moscow has increased economic and military aid to Hanoi to more than $6 billion per year. The annual interest payments on these debts alone exceed $360 million.

What, besides a vital strategic military presence, does Moscow expect in return for these massive amounts of assistance to Vietnam, assistance that Moscow itself can ill afford while in the throes of her own economic retrenchment? The answer is food, cheap labor (some describe it as slave labor), and oil exploration rights.

Over 60 percent of Vietnam's exports go to the Soviet Union. In the late 1970s, when there was an occasional Vietnamese agricultural surplus, most of that food was taken by Moscow, thus earning Vietnam the unflattering and insulting moniker Siberia's Greenhouse. Furthermore, to return the "Soviet favor," Hanoi has been shipping thousands of workers to Siberia to do manual labor. Selected for this disagreeable task have been thousands of former South Vietnamese soldiers and sympathizers. Mail received in the United States by relatives of these "guest workers" has indicated that they experience harsh working and living conditions, inadequate diet and medical care, and an uncertain future.

A Western visitor to Hanoi quickly notices the peculiar relationship between the Vietnamese people and visiting Soviets. Despite the fact that the Soviets are the only large nation to consistently provide much-needed assistance to the Vietnamese, and the fact that the Moscow-Hanoi relationship has lasted decades, there is an increasing unhappiness in the Vietnamese populace toward the Soviets. Indeed, a high-level Vietnamese official working in the foreign ministry confided to me that the Soviets are all housed "away from the Vietnamese people." The Soviet military advisers who work at either Danang or Cam Ranh Bay live in a compound or on board their ships. There is little contact between the Vietnamese population and the Soviets. Hanoi is probably afraid that many Vietnamese people, unhappy with the puny Soviet assistance for the Vietnamese people, will so insult the Soviets that Moscow will cut back on its aid.

As a Caucasian, I was repeatedly mistaken for a Soviet citizen as I walked around Hanoi. Barefoot children, wearing clothes held together by safety pins, would run up to me and shout, "Lien Xo!" (pronounced Lin So), meaning "Russian." This semi-insult was uttered with a tone of disdain. But when my interpreter corrected them and told them I was an American, smiles and a warm curiosity replaced the tension. One would think it would be the other way around: they should hate the Americans for bombing them during the war, and they should like the Soviets for being of help in a time of need. But in Vietnam, as elsewhere, a pushy Soviet character has shown through. The huge amount of Soviet aid is directed mostly for Soviet military purposes, as in the case of the invasion of Kampuchea. The Vietnamese people gain nothing from this.

The hunger, disease, lack of education, and decaying infrastructure have not been helped at all by the Soviets. Even Soviet nonmilitary assistance has, in many cases, proved to be a failure. The Soviet-designed hydroelectric dam, the Tri An Dam, was shut down just a week after it was first opened. This plant, designed to provide electricity for Ho Chi Minh City (formerly Saigon) was found to be defective. Not only are there problems in the turbine engines that caused power blackouts, but fear has spread through the populace living below the dam that it could fracture and give way. Inspections have shown that bad concrete and faulty welding are to blame. Even those in Moscow accept some of the criticism, citing their own inability to deliver needed materials on time.

After receiving more than $17 billion in combined military and economic assistance from Moscow, Vietnam's leaders have turned their eyes westward, specifically to the United States. The Deputy Foreign Minister, Nguyen Dy Nien, repeatedly talked to me of securing "American technology." The Vietnamese may be poor, but they are not dumb. They see the growing disparity between the Soviet bloc and the West when it comes to economic and scientific progress.

In fact, Minister Nien held a small dinner for me in the state house in Hanoi. During the evening, Nien and his subordinates questioned me about computers, television, Star Wars, medicine, and other American technological advances. They have nothing but admiration for American and Western accomplishments. (They also love American entertainment, especially football, Muhammad Ali, and even televised heavyweight wrestling.) What a shame that we don't use this advantage to wean Vietnam from Moscow.

## IV

Unlike the Soviet Union and China, Washington does not greet Vietnam's new government and new policies with a friendly ear. In fact, since the invasion of Kampuchea in late 1978, Vietnam has been branded an international pariah by the United States and other Western nations. This is perplexing, especially in light of the purpose of the Kampuchean operation: to remove Pol Pot's reign of terror, which threatened to go beyond Kampuchean borders into Vietnam and was perceived as a danger to Hanoi.

Pol Pot was compared to Adolph Hitler for the brutal execution of over two million of his own people. The foolishness of U.S. policy can be seen in our inconsistencies: the United States continues to legally recognize Pol Pot's Khmer Rouge as part of the legitimate tripartite representative of Kampuchea in the United Nations, but refuses to recognize the government of Vietnam. It makes no sense—and has not served U.S. interests.

In a new attempt to move toward the West, Hanoi has now offered a military and diplomatic carrot that could alter the strategic balance of the Pacific rim. At a time when the Philippines have made noises about not renewing the U.S. leases for the two vital bases there, Subic Bay and Clark Field, the possibility of the United States returning peacefully to Vietnam is astonishing.

Securing normalization of relations, the official welcoming back into the community of nations, is Hanoi's number one priority. The Vietnamese know that they cannot resuscitate their economy without Western economic assistance and trade. Hanoi cannot trade with these Western nations until Washington normalizes relations and lifts the trade embargo imposed on Vietnam after the Kampuchean invasion.

This trade embargo has caused Vietnam to lose millions of dollars of potential investment. For example, in 1987 Honda of Japan was prepared to build a large plant in Vietnam to manufacture motorbikes and car parts. This deal would have meant employment, training, and much-needed hard currency for Vietnam. But one U.S. senator, Robert Kasten (R-Wis.), rose on the Senate floor to protest this deal. Honda promptly withdrew, fearful of inciting an already protectionist-leaning Senate to take punitive steps toward Honda.

In this atmosphere, the new Hanoi government, led by economic reformers from the more free-enterprise-oriented and more prosperous south, as opposed to the older, more hard-line pro-Moscow group that prosecuted the war, has had to devise new approaches to convince Washington to normalize relations. It is appalling that the Reagan administration did not see the incredible value in assisting Vietnam in moving away from total dependence on the Soviet Union and that no one in the Reagan administration even talked to the Vietnamese leaders about the future status of the two former U.S. bases.

After the initial conversation in the backseat of the Volga limo, it did not take me long to ascertain a few vital facts from some other Hanoi officials. First, Cam Ranh Bay and Danang are not Soviet bases, as has often been reported in the West. It was carefully explained to me that both are Vietnamese bases, with the Soviets there as guests of the government of Vietnam. There is no formal approval of the Soviet presence by the Hanoi regime. In other words, it is a temporary arrangement between the leaders of Vietnam and the leaders of the Soviet Union. There is no treaty, no lease. Of course, that is not to say that Hanoi could or would just throw the Soviets out, but it is possible that Vietnam would make space available on each base for ships and planes of other nations, especially the United States. Such an arrangement would be similar to that in Cuba, where both the USSR and the United States base ships within a few miles of each other; those of the United States at Guantanimo and the Soviet Union's at Cienfuegos. And, cleverly, Hanoi dangles this carrot in Washington's face with one catch: it must come after relations are normalized between Hanoi and Washington.

The Reagan administration treated Vietnam with disdain, dispatching an insultingly low-level official to conduct talks with Hanoi's leaders. Besides the indignity of sending a junior ranking military officer to conduct diplomatic discussions, this man's lack of imagination and poor training prevented him from exploring with the Vietnamese ways to assist both countries.

The United States should first be interested in what is in U.S. interests. The possibility of weaning Vietnam from the Soviet Union is definitely in our interests. Certainly the potential return of U.S. forces to Cam Ranh Bay and Danang serves a multitude of U.S. objectives: (1) it neutralizes the Soviet presence in Vietnam, (2) it strengthens our hand in negotiations with the Philippines over the renewal of our leases there, and (3) it offers us a new beginning in Southeast Asia, one that will be welcomed by Japan, Indonesia, and Malaysia.

From Hanoi's perspective, the use of this carrot can satisfy Vietnam's two most pressing needs: it will cause the acceleration of the normalization of relations, and it will bring into Vietnam much-needed U.S. money. Hanoi's leaders are aware that Washington pays Manila more than $1 billion per year for the use of those two bases, not to mention the associated spending of up to another $1 billion. Vietnam's leaders are certain to use their newfound free-market approach to negotiate a comparable lease arrangement for the return of U.S. forces to Cam Ranh Bay and Danang. Of course, once this precedent is set, Hanoi can charge Moscow a similar rent and really be in the middle of some serious bidding.

## V

At a time when the Soviet Union has invested billions in expanding its Pacific presence, it is in the interest of the United States to offset that expansion. The U.S. flag once again flying at Cam Ranh Bay and Danang will send a strong signal throughout Asia and the Pacific that the United States is once again "in the game" in that region. Furthermore, once relations are normalized between Washington and Hanoi, U.S. economic prowess will triumph over the aggressive Soviet military presence. With Vietnam already considering market-oriented reforms, that country is ripe for Western economic suggestions and private assistance. With Moscow struggling with its own economic decline, the Soviets are in no position to compete for Vietnam or any other Third World country on an economic playing field; they have only the promise of increased military assistance. However, Hanoi is now less interested in war making; thus the decreased need for Moscow's assets.

Vietnam today is hoping to follow in China's footsteps and peacefully reform its economy. Whoever can help Hanoi the most in that goal, whether it be the USSR or the United States, will emerge victorious in winning the friendship of the new government of Vietnam.

The tragedy of U.S. policy under Ronald Reagan is not that the President of the United States considered the option in Vietnam, including a return to Cam Ranh Bay and Danang, and rejected it for certain well-considered reasons. No, the tragedy is that President Reagan was not even told of this latest option, because no one in the administration even knew about it. This frustration is shared by the new government in Hanoi, which repeatedly tried to communicate with the presidents but was continually intercepted by National Security Council (NSC) and Pentagon staffers who had their own agenda for Vietnam.

The Vietnamese are a persistent people; if nothing else, we should have learned that from their conduct during the war. They are not going to beg for better relations with Washington, nor should they have to. I commented on this when I had a long meeting with Vietnam's erudite and worldly deputy prime minister and foreign minister Nguyen Co Thach. "You are a proud people," I said as we shared traditional Vietnamese green tea. He replied enthusiastically in flawless English, "Yes, yes . . . you understand us well." The Vietnamese should be treated with respect, even if Washington disapproves of some of their policies. What makes no sense is to cut off all contact, thereby limiting our ability to gently influence Hanoi.

During the debate over placing sanctions on the government of South Africa, the argument was made that to pull back in our friendly relations with Pretoria would inevitably lead to less U.S. influence over that government. Thus was born the phrase "constructive engagement." The same applies elsewhere in the world. Regarding Vietnam, our policy for the last decade has been one of "destructive disengagement." By refusing to talk to Hanoi about anything except our concerns on Kampuchea and a few bilateral issues, we have helped to push Vietnam firmly into Moscow's grasp. Now we have a new opportunity to reverse the fortunes of Southeast Asia by neutralizing the growing Soviet presence there.

On November 2, 1987, Soviet General Secretary Mikhail Gorbachev extended his economic and political reform program, *perestroika,* to the field of foreign affairs. Speaking to foreign socialist delegates meeting in Moscow to commemorate the seventieth anniversary of the Bolshevik Revolution, Gorbachev attacked the "arrogance of omniscience" of previous Soviet regimes in dealing with the USSR's allies. Gorbachev added that such arrogance "speaks of a tenacious habit to reject other points of view out of hand."

Sitting in the audience that cold, gray day in Moscow was the new leader of Vietnam, Nguyen Van Linh. Certainly Gorbachev's words were not lost on this leader from the more free-enterprise-oriented south of Vietnam. General Secretary Linh must have seen the hypocrisy in the Soviet leader's clever speech, because, although Gorbachev denounced omniscience, his Soviet government continues to practice diplomacy through military omnipotence.

Chairman Linh, while not about to reject help from any quarter, including Moscow, soon returned to Hanoi convinced that the time was ripe to increase efforts at economic reform. The key ingredient in that plan was to improve relations with the United States. Thus, Linh and his new government have extended their hand of postwar friendship to Washington. The key question is whether Washington will accept that hand of friendship.

During my time in Hanoi, I met Le Cong Giao, a Vietnamese from the south who had escaped the Communists in 1975. Giao is now a U.S. citizen living in Los Angeles. We happened to stay in the same hotel in Hanoi. It was Giao's first trip back to his homeland since leaving thirteen years earlier. Each morning after breakfast, Giao would stroll out of the hotel to talk with passersby as they walked past the front door. One day, after an hour, he returned shaking his head with a look on his face which was a combination of sadness and bemusement. He pulled me aside and quietly repeated what a number of Vietnamese had just told him: things were so bad now in Vietnam that many of the people said, "We wish the Americans had won the war."

# 2

# THE NEW VIETNAM

## I

A new Vietnam was born in December 1986. The Vietnamese Communist party met in Hanoi to select a new government. After decades of rule by traditional, pro-Moscow, Marxist hard-liners, the Vietnamese opted for a new alternative. Following in the wake of China and the Soviet Union, the Vietnamese selected a new leader who recognized that, for all its wonderful-sounding rhetoric, socialism was a miserable economic failure. The new general secretary of the Communist party of the Socialist Republic of Vietnam was Nguyen Van Linh. He replaced the aging general secretary Truong Chinh, who, along with Premier Pham Van Dong, had run Vietnam since the 1969 death of the Vietnamese demigod, Ho Chi Minh. In a virtual clean sweep of old-timers, Pham Van Dong was retired. Also tossed aside in this major governmental shuffle was Le Duc Tho, who had won the 1973 Nobel Peace Prize for negotiating the Paris Peace Accords. Tho had long been a staunch supporter of the Soviet Union. These three elder statesmen were gently pushed offstage to be replaced by Linh and others, many of whom had experience in Vietnam's south, where they had learned that market-oriented economics worked better than rigid, state-planned Marxism.

Linh brought with him Vo Van Kiet, another southerner, as Chairman of the Council of Ministers. Kiet shared Linh's belief that for Vietnam to survive, drastic economic restructuring was necessary. Even Foreign Minister Nguyen Co Thach, while loyally serving the regime of Pham Van Dong, privately supported a new foreign and domestic policy that featured Western-style economic reforms. Thach had taken to studying the basic economic textbooks written by Milton Friedman and Paul Samuelson for U.S. college freshmen. Thus, with the advent of General Secretary Linh, Thach's inclinations were supported; he altered Vietnamese foreign policy to support Linh's domestic economic reforms. Primary in this new foreign policy was a focus on rapidly improving relations with the West, specifically with the United States. The Linh-Kiet-Thach group knew that the key to their economic reforms could be found only after Washington normalized relations, lifted the trade embargo, and unleashed the U.S. private sector to come and invest in developing nations like Vietnam.

Apparently the system of governmental checks and balances is not solely confined to Western constitutional democracies. Hanoi filled the post of Premier with Pham Hung, a long-time hard-liner who headed internal security, the group responsible for rounding up dissenters and consigning them to "reeducation camps." Hung represented those inside the Vietnamese government who differed with Linh not on the direction of policy but rather on the pace of reform. The Linh-Kiet-Thach group favored more rapid change.

Nguyen Van Linh has gone largely unnoticed by the Western press. A northerner by birth, the seventy-three-year-old general secretary has long been a dedicated Communist who, simultaneously, has had his eye on the United States. During the war, Linh was in charge of Communist propaganda in the south. He also became a self-taught expert on the U.S. presidential election process, once, as the story goes, boasting to colleagues that they had "defeated Johnson; . . . we can defeat Nixon, as well."

From his years living and working in the south, Linh saw the Western economic influences left behind after the U.S. withdrawal in 1975. Certainly there was a legacy of "decadent" social habits, including drugs and prostitution, that a Marxist found repellent, but there was also an economic fingerprint that differed sharply from that in Vietnam's north. Despite the Communist victory and the resulting purges and imprisonments in the south, a distinctively southern culture remained alive. A tradition and history of free-market capitalism, including profit making, banking, and economic sophistication, survived. However, in the north, after decades of constant war making, the Vietnamese could not adjust to a peace-time economy. Food shortages, inflation, and disease increased; productivity, foreign trade, and hard currency decreased.

In 1982 Nguyen Van Linh saw the rapidly deteriorating state of Vietnam's national economy. He advocated to his party comrades that some economic reforms were needed, along the lines of what had worked successfully in the south. He was promptly purged from the government. The Truong Chinh–Pham Van Dong–Le Duc Tho faction, stubborn to the point of economic suicide, would have no part of anything that deviated from traditional pro-Moscow Marxism. The determination, persistence, and arrogance that served North Vietnam so well during the war was killing Vietnam, economically, after the war.

From 1982 through 1986, the economic condition of Vietnam continued to disintegrate. Unable to grow enough rice to feed the Vietnamese population, Hanoi was forced to ask Moscow to give them rice. Disease ran rampant, as Vietnam had no access to modern medicine. The infrastructure continued to fall apart. Necessities such as fertilizer and other agricultural chemicals were unavailable, except inferior leftover brands from the Soviets.

Economically, Hanoi was ill prepared to cope with the task of running a peace-time economy. Generations trained in guerrilla warfare found themselves ill equipped to understand even the basics of currency devaluation and interest rates. Wracked by inflation, huge mounting debts to Moscow, and an inability to dig out from the ever-escalating unhappiness of the populace, especially in the more populous and productive south, the senior leaders of the party knew that changes must finally be made.

When, in December 1986, the aging Le Duc Tho and Pham Van Dong were gently retired and given positions as "advisers" to the party, they were cast aside. They had succeeded in their primary task in the 1970s: they had defeated the United States in the war and won independence. They had failed since, because in winning this independence, they had actually become almost totally dependent on Moscow.

For Nguyen Van Linh, his selection as the general secretary was a stunning victory, bringing him back from political exile. For Vietnam it was a startling departure from the past. The advent of

Linh and his cohorts would mean change across the board, in both domestic and foreign policy.

It did not take Vietnam's new leader long to symbolically demonstrate his new style. Just a few months after taking office, an unsigned newspaper column began to appear on the front page of Hanoi's largest daily paper, *Nham Dan*. This regular column was entitled "Things That Must Be Done Immediately" and contained an agenda for change for Vietnam, ranging from calls for the reduction of the government bureaucracy to more freedom for artists to criticize the government.

Old-timers and remaining hard-liners were shocked when it was revealed that this column was authored by Nguyen Van Linh. Who had ever heard of the leader of a Communist government not only publicly criticizing his own government, but also encouraging others to criticize the government? And criticize he did: General Secretary Linh launched a series of attacks against the size of the government payroll, calling bureaucrats "budget-eaters"; he sympathized with a group of artists who were afraid to speak out for fear of prosecution or an unwanted stay in a political reeducation camp; he said he understood their plight and felt, as they did, unable to speak freely. This will change, he implied.

The newspaper column was merely a symbol of Linh's desire to transform Vietnam from a dependent, decaying, poverty-stricken Third World nation that was considered to be one of the world's ten poorest countries into a truly independent, self-sustaining country able to be a player in Southeast Asia. The "things that must be done immediately" were (1) revitalize the domestic economy; (2) improve relations with the United States and the other Western economic powers, including Japan; and (3) attract foreign assistance, including technology, medical help, and outside industrial investment.

## II

Nguyen Van Linh was selected by his fellow Vietnamese communists to restore Vietnam's economy. Any Western visitor to Hanoi is shocked by the poverty, the misery, and the absolute lack of modern technology. The telephones only occasionally work, air conditioning is almost nonexistent, the roads are never repaired, and even buildings only ten years old are already decaying. A new bridge in Hanoi took years to finish because the Chinese withdrew assistance during the project, and Hanoi workers were incapable of picking up where the Chinese left off. At the airport, when an Air Vietnam commercial jetliner's front landing gear collapsed during a landing, the entire airport was closed until bureaucrats could figure out what to do; the plane itself remained in the middle of the runway for one entire day before it was towed to the side.

The situation is so miserable in Hanoi that any American is soon bound to ask, "How did the Vietnamese ever win the war?" One of the answers is that we misjudged and misunderstood the Vietnamese people. Their single most compelling national characteristic is a fierce, unyielding pride and desire to be independent of any outside force. It was this spirit that allowed them to survive almost unbearable personal hardship to win the war by waging a war of attrition.

Linh's task was to transfer this war-making spirit into productive economic enterprises. State-controlled centralized businesses were not producing even enough food to feed the population. Something had to be done.

In his first two years as general secretary, Linh has already begun reforms of many aspects of Vietnamese life. He has advocated decentralized control of business, with factories and agricultural units able to set their own economic goals. Private factories in the south are used as examples of how businesses should be run. A small flashlight factory in Saigon is touted as the model for private businesses.

Linh has moved to reduce governmental intervention in the lives of the people. A United Nations official stationed in Hanoi told me in March 1988, "In the one and a half years I have been here, there has been a noticeable lessening of the power of the state in the everyday lives of the people. It is still here, but it is lessening. You can see and feel it."

With a chronic lack of educated professionals who possess technological expertise, Linh also knows that he must attract foreign capital investment and the accompanying professionals who can train Vietnamese workers and managers. Perhaps Linh's most radical accomplishment in his first years in office has been the adoption of a new, liberal investment code designed to attract outside business investment, specifically Japanese and U.S. investment. This code provides that a foreign business can come to Vietnam and operate with the assurance that 100 percent of profits can be repatriated. The new code allows for joint Vietnamese-foreign business ventures, with the foreign entity supplying up to 99 percent of the equity. This new program also enables the foreign entity to bring in one of its own to run the operation. Management can hire and fire anyone it pleases.

Linh's hope is that his new investment program, one of the most lenient in the Communist world, will attract firms that will provide Vietnam with much-needed hard currency. Top priority is to be given to ventures that use high technology, develop natural resources, produce export goods, and develop Vietnamese industries, such as shipbuilding, manufacturing, and tourism.

While the Vietnamese hope to attract foreign investment, the home front continues to deteriorate. Now ranked as one of the ten poorest nations in the world, Vietnam's economy shows no sign of recovering. In fact, the opposite is the case. Because of economic mismanagement and disastrous decisions regarding currency devaluation, the domestic economy now suffers from 1000 percent inflation, a climbing exchange rate, a 100 percent increase in the price of gold, and a one hundred dollar per capita gross national product.

A food crisis presently envelops Vietnam. The government announced in March 1988 that the prospects for overcoming this situation were bleak. Said the state daily newspaper, *Nhan Dan* (March 21, 1988), "In the days ahead and in the pre-harvest months, the grain situation will become even more tense. Our country is a long way from solving the grain problem." The number of malnourished families increases. Why was this situation worsening, especially with Vietnam virtually at peace for the first time in decades? The paper cited problems with transportation, labor, and inadequate insecticides, fertilizer, and fuel.

From 1985 to 1988, while Vietnam's population continued to grow by more than one million people annually, the production of rice has stagnated at about eighteen million tons per year. Thus Vietnam is forced to import food to feed the people. But, with little hard currency or foreign exchange, the government is almost incapable of paying for these vital food imports.

Vietnamese assistant minister for economic affairs Vu Khoan wrote in *Nhan Dan* on March 21, 1988, "We are not yet starving, but food is the most acute problem we face." He said Vietnam's food production overall has actually deteriorated in the 1985-88 time period. In 1985, Vietnam produced 748 pounds of food per person; by 1988 it had dropped to 620 pounds per person. By late April 1988, Hanoi announced that some northern provinces were suffering from widespread starvation. After Washington denied Vietnam's request for emergency food aid, Hanoi secured some short-term assistance from the European Economic Community.

Even the future generations are beginning with huge educational handicaps. Vietnam is short of available classroom space for all grades, beginning with kindergarten. Thus, children are forced into double shifts, with one group attending school from 6:00 A.M. until noon, the other in the afternoon. Any Western visitor to Hanoi can't help but be moved by the sight of hundreds of small school children skipping down the street in the predawn light. Despite the poverty, the children are clean and well dressed, each carrying a book bag.

Similarly, college graduates and postgraduate candidates find inadequate books, equipment, and teachers. The Vietnamese want to send students to U.S. universities to study, yet this is presently banned by Washington's trade embargo. This situation verges on the insulting: Pham Binh, Hanoi's first ambassador to Indonesia and now ambassador to France, told me in Hanoi on March 17, 1988, that he had met the president of Tufts University, Dr. Jean Mayer, in Tokyo. So enamored of Binh's worldliness and experience was Mayer that he invited Binh to come teach for a year at Tufts. Then, as an afterthought, President Mayer asked if Binh could please come "under a different passport."

### III

Faced with this widespread domestic deterioration, Nguyen Van Linh has been forced to prioritize "things that must be done immediately." In order to accomplish the first, the repair of Vietnam's economy, the second, improving relations with the West, particularly the United States, is mandated. As soon as Linh took the reins of power, he made changes in each of the outstanding bilateral issues that have apparently kept the United States and Vietnam apart.

To begin, he announced to various visiting dignitaries, including Indonesian foreign minister Mochtar Kusumaatmadja, that the Vietnamese invasion of Kampuchea was "hurting Vietnam." Linh meant that the invasion had caused the diplomatic and economic isolation of Vietnam, not only from the ASEAN countries, but also from the United States and its allies. Mochtar's interpretation of this was that the Vietnamese had found it almost impossible to "swallow Kampuchea." Indeed, the Kampuchean invasion was always cited as the main stumbling block preventing normalized relations between Washington and Hanoi. Linh probably also meant that the financial cost of maintaining over 130,000 soldiers in Kampuchea was hurting Vietnam. In either case, one of Linh's top priorities was to end the invasion of Kampuchea as soon as possible. Thus, soon after taking office, he announced that Vietnam would withdraw its troops by 1990. By June 1988, Hanoi had already withdrawn one-third of its troops.

Linh also addressed the bilateral issues that U.S. representatives always raised to the Vietnamese: the full accounting of the prisoner of war (POW) and missing in action (MIA) issue; the resumption of the Orderly Departure Program for Vietnamese refugees wishing to come to the United States; the emigration of the thousands of Amerasian children to America; and the release from prison camps of political prisoners, many of whom had worked for the United States during the war. On each of these issues, the Linh regime offered a new policy.

On the emotionally charged POW/MIA issue, Washington offered something new before Linh did. In March 1987, less than three months after assuming office, Linh was advised by a visiting American that President Reagan was soon to dispatch a special presidential emissary on the POW/MIA issue to Hanoi. This special envoy was to be retired general John Vessey, the former chairman of the Joint Chiefs of Staff. In April, public announcement of this appointment was made by the State Department, with one caveat:

Vessey would venture to Hanoi only after Hanoi received Lt. Col. Richard Childress from the National Security Council. Childress's trip was to set the agenda for Vessey, and Washington's terms were simple: there would be no linkage of progress on the POW/MIA issue and the granting of normalized relations by Washington.

So, without doing anything, Linh was confronted by a new cosmetic approach by Washington. Vessey visited Hanoi in August. He offered Vietnam a vague promise of "non-governmental organizational aid" but no direct assistance from Washington. It took the Vietnamese the entire year of 1987 to determine whether or not the "Vessey Initiative" would lead to better relations. Finally, in January 1988, after almost a year of waiting, Vietnamese Foreign Minister Nguyen Co Thach announced in a Hanoi press conference that it had abandoned the Vessey Initiative. "I can accept some private aid," said Thach, "but there has to be some direct help from the American government, as well."

By late August 1988, Hanoi had agreed to a new U.S. proposal calling for "joint Vietnamese-American searches" of U.S. crash sites outside Hanoi. For the first time, the Vietnamese government allowed U.S. technical teams to venture outside the capital city to interview citizens and excavate the remnants of U.S. aircraft. Vietnam also agreed to resolve the seventy "discrepancy" cases presented by General Vessey in August 1987. These are cases of U.S. soldiers known to have been captured alive but never heard of again.

On the remaining bilateral issues, however, Linh acted instead of reacted. For example, after less than one year in office, he announced that the political prisoners held in "re-education camps" were being released; by the end of 1987, supposedly only twenty-five hundred of the hundreds of thousands originally locked up remained incarcerated. On the Amerasian children issue, Vietnam announced willingness to let them all out and blamed the delay in emigrating to the United States on Washington. To break the logjam, Hanoi requested a U.S. governmental representative to come to Vietnam to discuss the issue. Washington refused. On the Orderly Departure Program, designed to facilitate the emigration of Vietnamese to the United States, Linh also has accelerated the pace of emigration. If, as some charge, the Vietnamese are playing games with emigration in order to secure concessions from Washington, what is strange about that? Is that not exactly what goes on vis-à-vis the Soviets and the Americans on the issue of Soviet Jews and dissidents?

Packaging all of these new approaches into a new public relations campaign, the Linh forces have made an unprecedented attempt to sell the New Vietnam to the American people. Present U.S. government officials and former government officers, ranging from Cyrus Vance to former members of Congress, have visited Vietnam. U.S. veterans groups, television and newspaper reporters, and college students are also welcome in every-increasing numbers in Vietnam. Even former president Richard Nixon was quietly invited by the Vietnamese government to visit Hanoi. He refused.

Undoubtedly Linh is drawing upon his background during the war as a self-educated expert on the U.S. political process. The key to the north's victory in the war had been the ability or luck of its leaders in allying themselves with the American political Left. This alliance had been just strong enough to puncture a weak Lyndon Johnson in New Hampshire in 1968, and, during the Nixon years, it had been successful in eroding American patience with the long, drawn-out war. However, Hanoi reads the American Left as much more powerful than it is. Today, Linh is hoping to form a new alliance, not just with the American Left, but with the American Center and Right, in hopes of convincing the administration to change its policy toward Vietnam. This explains the selling of the New Vietnam.

Despite these positive steps, the new Linh regime has been met in Washington with silence. No attempts have been made by Washington to seize the initiative and reciprocate with new initiatives. At a time when Gorbachev is lessening the Soviet Union's control over its allies, it is a tragedy that the United States does not reenter the diplomatic game in Southeast Asia and try to wean Vietnam from Moscow.

## IV

On March 10, 1988, the Vietnamese prime minister, Pham Hung, suddenly died of a massive heart attack. A hard-liner out of the old school, Hung had been in charge of Vietnamese internal security since the end of the war. It was this network of agents that was responsible for rounding up people who opposed Hanoi's rigid state-controlled programs and throwing them into reeducation camps. Pham Hung's original selection as prime minister in December 1986 was viewed as a check on Nguyen Van Linh's appointment as Communist party general secretary. There clearly was a continuing split in the Communist leadership between the ardently pro-Moscow group and the Linh forces, who preferred a new approach that incorporated some capitalist economic reforms.

A good measure of Linh's continuing power can be seen in the events immediately following Hung's death. Before the three-day national mourning period began, Linh engineered the appointment of one of his closest confidants, Vo Van Keit, as acting prime minister. As chairman of the Council of Ministers, Kiet has vigorously supported Linh's reforms; in fact, he had been Linh's choice in December 1986 to become prime minister. This time, however, Linh marshaled enough support to at least get Kiet in the post temporarily. In June 1988 the Vietnamese Communist party held its annual congress and selected Do Muoi to be the new premier. Muoi is known as a strict disciplinarian who was responsible for implementing socialism in the south after the war. However, he is now a supporter of Linh's reforms. His role may be to enforce these changes on a reluctant party bureaucracy.

The governmental struggle in Vietnam is not so simple as choosing to be pro-Moscow or pro-Western. Rather, it is one of determining the pace of reforms. Almost all of the Hanoi leadership recognizes the necessity of making fundamental economic changes; they disagree, though, on the speed and timing of these reforms. The Linh crowd wants to move more quickly than do the remnants of the hard-liners. A similar split is evidenced in Moscow between the forces loyal to General Secretary Gorbachev and those who prefer the slower pace advocated by Minister Igor Ligachev.

Now, while Linh's power is at its apex, is the correct time for the United States to move toward Hanoi. If Washington misses this opportunity, it is possible that two different scenarios could ensue: (1) Linh could be dumped for failure to reverse the economic downslide and replaced by a new generation hard-liner who is not as interested in improving relations with the United States; or (2) Japan and other Asian nations could begin to heavily invest in and trade with Vietnam, cornering the Vietnamese markets, cutting out the United States, and earning the friendship of Linh's forces. Both cases are distinct possibilities. A bold new step now by Washington could prevent these scenarios and instead insure a warm new relationship between Vietnam and the United States.

For those who imagine Vietnam to be a national Gulag, I must recount an incident from my trip to Hanoi in March 1988. Two officials from the foreign ministry took me forty miles outside Hanoi to visit the famed Perfume Pagoda, which is a large cave high up a mountain. It was a Sunday and I was struck by the thousands of Vietnamese of all ages determinedly hiking up the slippery, steep mountainside to reach a cave. They had come from all over Vietnam on their annual vacation trip. When we got to the Pagoda, I asked my guide, "Why are the people coming here?"

He replied simply, "They come to pray."

After a moment I dared to ask, "But I thought this was a communist state. I thought there was no religion . . . no praying."

My Vietnamese counterpart chuckled as he lit some incense to place inside the cave, "The state may not pray, but the people do."

# 3

# CHINA, ASEAN, AND KAMPUCHEA

## I

The present refusal by the U.S. government to even consider normalizing relations with Vietnam is based on two preconditions: (1) Hanoi must withdraw all its troops from Kampuchea, and the Kampuchean people must then be allowed to select their own government; and (2) Hanoi must provide a full accounting of lost U.S. servicemen (POWs and MIAs). This policy was adopted originally under the Carter administration after the Vietnamese invasion of Kampuchea in December 1978.

The Reagan administration followed the same policy, despite ample evidence that the policy actually accomplished none of Washington's goals and, in fact, was counterproductive. This hard line did not force Hanoi out of Kampuchea, and it did not bring about any substantive progress on the POW or the MIA issues. It merely served to isolate Vietnam and force it into Moscow's orbit.

As is often the case in Washington, policy is thrown together in a piecemeal fashion, with no desire to be consistent. For example, Vietnam's neighbor, Laos, has over five hundred cases of either known POWs or MIAs still unresolved. Laos is also a close ally of the Soviet Union, Vietnam, and the pro-Hanoi government in Kampuchea. However, none of this has prevented the United States from maintaining normalized relations with the Laotians.

Similarly, in the late fall of 1987, President Ronald Reagan excused the Soviet invasion of Afghanistan by saying that it was not

Gorbachev's problem because "he was not in office when it took place." The same argument can be applied to Vietnam's invasion of Kampuchea. Vietnamese Communist party General Secretary Nguyen Van Linh was not only not in office in 1978 at the time of the invasion, he was actually thrown out of government entirely in 1982. Furthermore, when he was brought back and given the highest post in his country, he immediately criticized the continuing presence of Vietnamese troops in Kampuchea. He has pledged to remove all Vietnamese troops by 1990.

While President Reagan encouraged a wave of superpower euphoria to sweep the United States, his administration continued to freeze Vietnam out of the community of nations. While the administration led the charge to increase private sector trade with Moscow, to the tune of over $10 billion per year, the trade embargo on Hanoi continued. And, during a period when we apparently decided to deal with Moscow in hopes of modifying their expansionist behavior, we refused to send anyone more prestigious to Hanoi than an army lieutenant colonel who served on the National Security Council staff.

## II

In October 1978, President Jimmy Carter was on the verge of an Asian diplomatic doubleheader: the normalization of relations with both China and Vietnam. However, bitter infighting among the State Department's assistant secretary for Asian and Pacific Affairs, Richard Holbrooke; the secretary of state, Cyrus Vance; and the White House national security advisor, Zbigniew Brzezinski, scuttled the recognition of Vietnam. Only China received full normalized relations. Less than two months later, in December, the Vietnamese dispatched over 150,000 combat troops into neighboring Kampuchea to eliminate the Khmer Rouge forces led by the Hitler of the 1970s, Pol Pot. From 1975 until late 1978, Pol Pot butchered over two million Kampuchean people. He destroyed his country and made threatening sounds toward Hanoi. His forces invaded Vietnam, killing over thirty thousand people, purposefully butchering babies and pouring their blood into the Mekong River until the river ran red. Some Khmer Rouge detachments ventured as far as the outskirts of Ho Chi Minh City (formerly Saigon).

Vietnam has ever been wary of its long, exposed western border. It has always desired friendly governments in both Laos and Kampuchea. To the leaders in Hanoi, Pol Pot's unprecedented slaughter of innocent Kampuchean civilians was repulsive. The threat to Vietnam, however, was unacceptable. The decision to invade was not a difficult one.

Almost ten years later, in 1988, Vietamese leaders privately insist that, had the United States normalized relations in October 1978, Hanoi would not have invaded Kampuchea. Of course, no one will ever know if this is true. But clearly, the Vietnamese view Washington's rejection in 1978 as a major setback for their development in the late 1970s. In the minds of the Vietnamese, they won their war. There was no need for the United States and Vietnam to remain in a virtual state of war. Why not work together in Southeast Asia, just as postwar Japan and the United States have done?

As the United States was rejecting Vietnam, Moscow was aggressively moving to fill the vacuum. Less than a month after Washington's decision not to normalize relations, the Soviet Union signed the friendship treaty with Hanoi. Under this agreement, Moscow began to make large military and nonmilitary loans available to a financially strapped Vietnam, with generously low interest rates and pay-back terms. The price for this unusual Soviet generosity was twofold: (1) access to the Vietnamese military facilities at Cam Ranh Bay and Danang, and (2) pressure from Moscow on Hanoi to invade Kampuchea, in order to carry out the Soviets' Asian master plan of encircling China with pro-Moscow proxies.

Undoubtedly Hanoi felt a legitimate threat along its borders from Pol Pot and may well have invaded Kampuchea on its own, but the rejection from Washington, combined with Soviet pressure, encouraged Hanoi to launch its invasion.

The reaction to this operation was explosive. Vietnam's Southeast Asian neighbors, including ASEAN, bitterly condemned Hanoi's decision. So did the United States. Vietnam's diplomatic campaign to be accepted among Western and other non-Communist nations was irrevocably set back. Hanoi quickly became an international pariah.

In retrospect, many argue that Vietnam performed a public service in removing Pol Pot and ending the wholesale barbarism of the Khmer Rouge. Oddly, the United States today still recognizes Pol Pot as the legitimate representative of Kampuchea in the United Nations. Washington's new friendly relationship with Beijing, Pol Pot's financier and protector, also reinforces the inconsistencies of U.S. foreign policy.

Whatever the cause ten years ago, the Kampuchean situation has become enmeshed in the continuing Soviet-Sino conflict and is, simultaneously, the product of a centuries-old contradictory relationship between China and Vietnam. Only the positive introduction of a new player, the United States, into the region can untie this messy, complicated knot.

## III

China and Vietnam, once as close as "lips and teeth," suffered a political break in 1978 after Hanoi's decision to invade Kampuchea. This Soviet-supported operation was seen in Beijing not only as a Vietnamese threat to China's eventual hegemony in the region, but also as a part of the Soviet strategy in the Pacific. Thus, the Chinese adopted a new regional policy with four main objectives: (1) weakening and isolating Vietnam; (2) preventing Vietnamese hegemony over Kampuchea and, possibly, Laos; (3) containing Soviet influence in the region; and (4) preventing the Association of Southeast Asian Nations from reaching an accommodation with Vietnam.

Beijing became the main financial and military supplier of the Khmer Rouge forces of Pol Pot. As the war in Kampuchea bogged down, the Chinese leader, Deng Xiaoping, according to Gareth Porter in an April 1987 article in *Current History,* said "It was wise for China to force the Vietnamese to stay in Cambodia because that way they will suffer more and more." Of course, this has been an accurate prediction. Because of the continued stalemate in Kampuchea, Vietnam has been severely set back in its campaign to restore relations with the West, Japan, and the thriving ASEAN nations. For this, China is happy. The growing Soviet military presence in Kampuchea, however, does not please Beijing.

At a meeting of Peking's Political Bureau the Chinese strategy for the eventual domination of Southeast Asia was explicitly detailed in 1965 by Mao Tse Tung: "We are bound to recover South-east Asia, which includes South Vietnam, Thailand, Burma, Malaysia and Singapore. Southeast Asia is very rich in minerals and to recover it is worth all the efforts we make. This region will be advantageous to China's future industrial development, and will make up for the losses. The east wind will prevail over the west wind when we have recovered Southeast Asia."

The fundamental break between China and the Soviet Union in the 1960s manifested itself during the Vietnam War. As early as 1963 the Chinese tried to forestall Moscow's presence in Southeast Asia. Then party secretary-general Deng offered Vietnam $250 million in financial aid with only one condition: Vietnam must reject all Soviet aid. Hanoi, long distrustful of reliance on only one outside power, refused the offer.

From that time onward, the Beijing-Hanoi relationship deteriorated. In 1965, Mao Tse Tung publicly announced to the United States, "Chinese troops will not cross their [Vietnam's] frontiers. China will fight only if it is attacked by America." Vietnamese leaders felt then that these statements tacitly encouraged U.S. political leaders to continue the war.

Simultaneously, Mao began his Cultural Revolution. Hanoi felt this was too radical a departure from traditional Marxism. Furthermore, the Vietnamese felt that Mao's overall strategy was for Vietnam to fight the war until it was exhausted, leaving Southeast Asia for Beijing's eventual domination. In June 1973 Mao told visiting Vietnamese leaders, "Frankly speaking, the Chinese people, the Chinese Communist party, and the world's people must thank the Vietnamese people for having defeated the U.S. aggressors. It was your victory, comrades, that forced Nixon to come to China." Hanoi's leaders resented the fact that they fought the United States, and the Chinese reaped the rewards.

Even though Mao refused to send Chinese troops to assist the Vietnamese against the French and the United States, Beijing did provide Hanoi with over $20 billion in financial assistance in the 1950s, 1960s and 1970s. In the end, however, China ended up not with a grateful ally but with a resolute enemy on its southern border.

In the mid-1970s, after the U.S. withdrawal from Saigon, Vietnam moved closer to the Soviets. At the same time, China and the

United States grew closer. With U.S. support, Beijing branded Vietnam as the "Cuba of Asia." And when Soviet proxies, in the form of 150,000 Vietnamese troops, invaded Kampuchea, Deng had to react. After preaching that Soviet expansionism must be checked, the Chinese were now faced with an example of it on their own southern border. In February 1979, the Chinese crossed into Vietnamese territory to "punish" Hanoi. This invasion lasted just four weeks. During that time, the Vietnamese soldiers, hardened by decades of continual warfare, soundly repelled the numerically superior Chinese forces. The Vietnamese used chemical weapons and inflicted severe casualties. However, from Beijing's point of view, the operation was a strategic success because Moscow had not come to its ally's rescue with Soviet troops. Thus, the Chinese had Moscow's measure. The Soviets would financially and militarily support Hanoi; they would not put Soviet troops into combat in Southeat Asia.

With the Chinese not willing to enter Kampuchea to wage direct war on Vietnam, and with Vietnam having routed the Khmer Rouge, stalemate ensued in Kampuchea. Beijing chose the course of an economic isolation of Vietnam, cutting Hanoi off from all outside assistance, save from Moscow. In order for this approach to be successful, China had to have the support of the United States, Japan, and the ASEAN states. In the late 1970s and early 1980s there was nearly unanimous approval for the economic embargo on Vietnam. Of course, the primary beneficiary of this isolation of Vietnam was Beijing. With Hanoi cut off from the world business community, bleeding economically at home, and tied down in a costly war in Kampuchea, it was in no position to prevent an eventual domination of Southeast Asia by China.

The selection of Nguyen Van Linh as the new leader of Vietnam presaged the breaking of this stalemate. As noted above, one of Linh's first priorities has been to withdraw Vietnamese troops from Kampuchea. He also is extending a hand of friendship to the United States, despite the fact, as he put it in an interview in *Time Magazine* "that America tried to bomb us back to the Stone Age." What Linh's associates hope for is to play their own "China card," once the United States has diplomatically reentered the region as a major player.

China under Mao may have wanted to dominate the entire Southeast Asia region; China under Deng has more immediate concerns, including domestic economic development and the Soviet military threat. The reentry of the United States into the region, manifested by the normalization of relations between Hanoi and Washington, will begin the process of neutralizing the Soviet military presence in both Vietnam and Kampuchea. It is in the interests of China, Vietnam, and the United States to reduce the Soviet military presence in the region. The key lies in Washington waking up from its fifteen-year funk and reasserting itself as a world superpower.

## IV

In the late 1960s, as the U.S. involvement in the Vietnam War peaked, the surrounding nations, including Thailand, Indonesia, Malaysia, Singapore, and the Philippines, correctly foresaw the eventual departure of a war-weary United States. In preparation for the ensuing vacuum, these nations, later joined by tiny but rich Brunei, created the Association of Southeast Asian Nations.

When, in 1975, the United States did withdraw from South Vietnam, ASEAN asserted itself as a combined force against the newly consolidated Vietnamese Communist government. However, it was not until the 1978 invasion of Kampuchea that ASEAN took an aggressive position against Hanoi. Echoing the fears of one of its member nations, Thailand, ASEAN denounced the invasion as a first step on a planned Vietnamese march across Indochina all the way to Malaysia. ASEAN demanded a Vietnamese pullout before improvement of relations with ASEAN or its member states could take place.

At the same time, the ASEAN countries began to prosper. Through a combination of mining, manufacturing, oil drilling, fishing, and clever marketing, these nations have grown in economic power. Today, ASEAN constitutes the United States' fifth largest trading partner. The United States has a close relationship to most of the nations in the organization, especially Thailand and the Philippines.

After the United States' humiliation in Vietnam, Washington turned its attention to the Middle East, Europe, and arms reductions with the Soviet Union; Washington abdicated any primary responsibility for events in Southeast Asia. The ASEAN countries naturally filled the void, with the United States happy to endorse whatever policy its friends adopted. This was incorrect behavior for a nation like the United States. For America to sit around moping over the war was bad enough; to subjugate itself to that of smaller regional powers was a mistake.

By the mid-1980s, the ASEAN countries were themselves deviating from the official policy of ASEAN. That policy was to embargo all trade with Hanoi until there was a Vietnamese withdrawal from Kampuchea and a government selected by the Kampuchean people. Like the tail wagging the dog, Washington followed in lock step, adopting the ASEAN policy as its own. Furthermore, Washington continued to refuse to normalize relations with Hanoi until they withdrew from Kampuchea. Meanwhile, some of the individual states within ASEAN began to violate their association's policy. In a stereotypically Asian way, Thailand and Singapore began to conduct extensive under-the-table trade with Vietnam. They, along with Malaysia and Indonesia, have normalized diplomatic relations with Vietnam. Manila, as well, has stepped up an always-friendly relationship with Hanoi.

Indeed, it is only Washington that is left in the dust, mouthing the official ASEAN Policy, while the individual ASEAN countries and Japan get a leg up on trading with Vietnam. This deterioration of U.S. position is a direct result of the abdication of responsibility at the end of the war in 1975. Allowing ASEAN to speak for the United States was a tactical mistake; letting the ASEAN nations jump ahead of us was a strategic blunder.

The only remedy now is to sidestep ASEAN and boldly forge a new relationship with Hanoi. The first step in this new relationship should be the normalization of relations between Washington and Hanoi, whether or not Vietnam has withdrawn its troops from Kampuchea.

In 1988, Secretary of State George Shultz announced that "The situation on the ground" is the best determinant of what our policy should be. Employing that test, it is inevitable that Hanoi will never allow Kampuchea to fall under the control of Pol Pot or the Khmer Rouge. Who can blame them? So why should Washington demand the impossible? Hanoi may very well withdraw its troops from Kampuchea, and Hanoi may tolerate a coalition government not to its liking. But certainly Hanoi cannot allow the Khmer Rouge to return to power. Thus, Washington should use its newfound influence with Beijing to pressure the Chinese to cut off Chinese financial and military support for Pol Pot. That step, along with U.S. diplomatic recognition of Vietnam, would quickly place the United States once again at the epicenter of events throughout Asia.

The United States needs to see the bigger picture in Southeast Asia and try to change it in this country's best interests. The normalization of relations should be the first in a series of steps taken to offset the growing Soviet influence in the region, as well as to allow the United States to compete with its ASEAN friends, who have used Washington as a mouthpiece for too long. From now on, the United States must realize that, while the ASEAN states are friends of America, they are also our competitors. Why should we stay out of the region and allow them a monopoly on the trade potential with Vietnam? We should not.

# V

Asia is the model of the world's diplomatic future. Alliances serve mutual interests; yet one's enemy can also be one's partner. Shifting, floating relationships are a constant. In Asia more than anywhere else, nations can be angry with each other publicly, but carry on a widespread private business relationship.

The United States is to slow to adapt to this new rule of diplomacy. We are just now realizing that even in Europe, the North Atlantic Treaty Organization (NATO) is a paper tiger; it has been supplanted by the individual Western European nations making their own arrangements with each other—and with the common adversary who originally caused the formation of NATO: the Soviet Union. For Washington, the opening of relations with Beijing is the only adaptation to this new diplomacy in the past two decades; all the other changes are reactions to the fall of a U.S. friend or ally.

The United States in the 1980s has focused, correctly, on rebuilding its domestic economy and its military forces. However, Washington has ignored how to use these two revitalized U.S. assets. Diplomacy is not the process of dispatching some well-dressed former college professor to lecture and berate another nation's foreign minister; diplomacy is the art of using carrots and sticks. Foreign economic aid and private trade are the carrots; the threat of military force, the presence of those forces, or the imposition of trade and economic sanctions are potential sticks. The shrewd use of these incentives and threats are the ground rules of successful diplomacy. The United States has all but ignored the correct usage of these assets in Southeast Asia.

U.S. leaders should learn the other basic rule of diplomacy; that whatever a foreign government may say in public is not necessarily what that same government will say, or do, in private. The need for national leaders to play politics for domestic consumption is sometimes a necessary evil. Even Communist, totalitarian governments in which the public has no direct say in the selection of leaders or the policies those leaders adopt, adhere to this diplomatic tradition. In these one-party, nondemocratic nations, the leaders still compete for their power and thus find it necessary to say things at home that may differ from what they actually will do.

With this rule in mind, it should be a necessity for the United States not only to have normal diplomatic relations with Hanoi, but also to step up U.S. intelligence gathering and study of the Indochina nations. I was shocked in 1986 when I visited then CIA director William Casey and two top CIA experts on Southeast Asia. None of these officials could even give me the correct name of the three leaders of Laos, a nation with which we do have normalized relations. I was equally disappointed that same year when, in a discussion at the State Department, Deputy Secretary of State John C. Whitehead asked his top lieutenant, "Do we have an embassy in Hanoi?"

When the so-called experts don't even know the names of the leaders of these Asian nations or whether or not we have relations with them, how can these same officials possibly recommend sound policy alternatives to our elected officials? Of course they can't. That is one of the reasons why our policy in Southeast Asia has caused us to become the "forgotten superpower," basically a nonplayer in the world's most rapidly growing region.

The debate over a relatively simple step such as normalizing relations with Vietnam should not consume a decade. Indeed, a debate should and will ensue over subsequent policies, especially those including any direct payments of public funds to Vietnam. However, the Constitution grants the power to recognize a nation solely unto the president of the United States; congressional approval is not required. Perhaps the Founding Fathers were correct; this type of decision should not require a national debate.

## VI

As we head into a new century, the world's number one growth area will continue to be the Pacific region. Many U.S. businessmen have foreseen this and shifted their emphasis from Europe to Asia. Certainly the Soviets know this; their vast military and commercial shipping buildup demonstrates their new emphasis on being a "Pacific nation." Japan is investing throughout the Pacific rim all the way to Hawaii and America's West Coast. Recently, Tokyo floated the proposal to invest $4 billion in Vietnam; Washington immediately protested.

Oddly, the United States, a legitimate Pacific power, built on the notion of moving westward in an ever-searching quest for new areas, new markets, and new horizons, now has a government that follows a cryptoisolationist policy in this crucial part of the Pacific.

Bitter over the disaster of losing the Vietnam War, the U.S. government refuses to let go of the past and recognize the changes occurring daily in Southeast Asia. The long-term cost to the United States will be great if Washington does not change. We face the possibility of being shut out of this potentially rich economic area. Furthermore, without the steadying hand of the United States, either the Soviets or the Chinese could overrun or overly influence this area.

There is no logical explanation or defense for present U.S. policy on Southeast Asia. However, many Americans believe there are other ugly remnants of the Vietnam War besides a bad foreign policy. One of those remaining issues, that of the living U.S. prisoners of war, may help to explain the reasons for the United States' ill-conceived and illogical policy.

# 4

# PAWNS IN THE GAME BETWEEN WASHINGTON AND HANOI

## I

Since the late 1970s, the intelligence reports coming out of Vietnam and Laos have been strikingly similar in describing American prisoners of war still held against their will. The men are kept in small groups, anywhere from six to twelve. They are not held in a conventional prison setting; instead, they are moved frequently about the countryside to prevent fraternization with the local population and to avoid predictable schedules that would facilitate a rescue mission. They are forced to work. Before their capture, most of these Americans were pilots, officers, electrical engineers, or radar experts, and most are college graduates.

In a region of the world where most people are poor and illiterate, these men are storehouses of technical knowledge. Thus, these prisoners are forced to repair helicopter engines, fix radar installations, build airstrips, teach English, and inoculate livestock. Who better to repair and refurbish the $4 billion worth of U.S. military equipment abandoned by the United States in 1975 with the fall of Saigon? They live, under guard, in caves or locked inside bamboo cages. In some cases, the Americans held in the remote sections of Laos are relatively free to roam about their villages because in these desolate areas there are no footpaths or roads. Outsiders arrive only on one of the thrice-monthly Pathet Lao Army helicopter flights. A few of the POWs have been allowed to form relationships with local women.

From these intelligence reports, many conclude that these American POWs are, in fact, twentieth-century slaves, for they are the property of and work for their captors. These men are held inside Laos, but they are "owned" by Vietnam and guarded by soldiers responsive to Hanoi. Vietnam continues to claim that there are no American POWs in Vietnam. Technically, that is correct.

The Vietnamese, however, do not always conceal. In late 1987, a high Vietnamese official met privately in New York with me, knowing that I have long been involved with the cause of the POWs of the Vietnam War. This Vietnamese official said that Americans must learn one thing: "You don't give, you don't get."

Of all the issues between Hanoi and Washington, the question of POWs—the question of giving and getting—hangs over any discussion. Vietnam has used, and still is using, the giving and getting of the POW issue to blackmail the U.S. government. The United States wants its soldiers, sailors, and airmen returned. Vietnam wants diplomatic recognition and economic assistance.

Not all Americans, however, want to negotiate for the POWs. In the United States, the POW issue is replete with lies, duplicity, and falsifications by the executive branch, by Congress, and by the media. For example, fearful of a critical and hostile public reaction to the truth about the original abandonment of the POWs and about their continued detention in Southeast Asia, some in the U.S. intelligence community have waged a campaign inside the executive branch to hide the truth.

Thus, in the late 1980s, as one result of this campaign, some Americans wonder if it is possible that U.S. servicemen are still being held in Vietnam or somewhere else in Communist Indochina. Why, they ask, would Hanoi hold these men? Why would Hanoi claim they are not holding any American POWs? Certainly the intelligence agencies in Washington must know by now if there are any POWs in Southeast Asia. Why has the U.S. government failed to bring these men home?

As these questions suggest, any improvement in relations between Vietnam and Washington will not occur until the repatriation of American POWs is no longer seen as a threat to both governments. Hanoi, in part, attributes its victory in the war to the ability to influence U.S. public opinion. Hanoi does not want to antagonize the American people, but what will they feel if Hanoi gives up these prisoners after all these years? Washington, on the other hand, has at best been delinquent for not pressing hard enough to obtain a settlement and has at worst deliberately covered up the truth about the POWs in Southeast Asia.

The return of American POWs, choreographed for national television, will ignite a public firestorm of protest—not only against Hanoi for holding the men but also against Washington for doing so little. A resolution, however, to this vexing problem can bring these two former enemies into an amicable relationship. Then the balance of power in Southeast Asia will move away from Moscow.

## II

The first attempt to resolve the POW issue took place on January 27, 1973, the day the Paris Peace Accords were signed. Since the signing, the Vietnamese have publicly denied holding any American POWs other than those covered in that document. Under the terms of that agreement, Hanoi pledged to return to the United States 591 prisoners captured during the war. In the next two months, in four installments, Vietnam did release these prisoners.

The Paris Peace Accords contained two sections that, for years later, were central to solving the POW question and explain why Hanoi and Washington remain so far apart. Section 8B of the accords states, "The parties shall help each other to get information about those military personnel and foreign civilians of the parties missing in action." Section 21 stated that the United States "would contribute to the healing of the wounds of war." While those were two sections among many, soon the two were to be forever intertwined in a clever Vietnamese gambit to secure massive economic assistance from the United States. From that day on, Hanoi has steadfastly linked progress on the POW question to direct United States economic assistance to Hanoi.

Five days after signing the accords, both sides again met in Paris to exchange a letter from President Richard Nixon in return for a Vietnamese list of American POWs alive in Laos. These prisoners were not covered by the Paris accords. In other words, Hanoi contended that the POWs in Laos were not held in a system under Vietnamese control. (Laos was, at that time, divided between the pro-Western Royal Lao and the Hanoi-backed Pathet Lao. The American prisoners in question were allegedly held by the Pathet Lao.) Furthermore, Laos was not a party to the Paris accords.

The February 1, 1973, letter from Nixon to Premier Minister Pham Van Dong stated, "The Government of the United States of America will contribute to postwar reconstruction in North Vietnam without any political preconditions." How much would the United States contribute? According to the Nixon letter, "preliminary United States' studies indicate that the appropriate programs for the United States contribution to postwar reconstruction will fall in the range of $3.25 billion in grant aid over five years. Other forms of aid will be agreed upon between the two parties." The "other forms" of aid were touched upon later in Nixon's letter: "In regard to other forms of aid, United States studies indicate that the appropriate programs could fall in the range of $1 to $1.5 billion depending on food and other commodity needs of the Democratic Republic of Vietnam." (See Appendix A.)

Thus, five days after signing the Paris Peace Accords, the United States had agreed to an unconditional grant of up to $4.75 billion over a five-year period to Hanoi. In return for this pledge, Hanoi handed the United States representative in Paris a list of Americans held in Laos. Clearly these events, the pledging of money to Hanoi and the listing of POWs in Laos, established an all-important linkage: the release of American POWs in Laos was linked to the payment of money to Hanoi.

Although little was then or has since been written about the U.S. war in Laos, it was acknowledged by all sides at that time that many U.S. fliers and soldiers were being held prisoner by the Pathet Lao. Hanoi acknowledged them. A spokesman for the Pathet Lao admitted their presence in early February 1973. Washington acknowledged them as well. In fact, as soon as the list was handed over by the Vietnamese to the Americans and cabled to Washington, the Pentagon reacted with dismay. The list contained only ten names! "It doesn't appear to us that this could be a complete list and we are asking some questions through diplomatic channels," said Pentagon spokesman Jerry Friedheim in *Pacific Stars and Stripes*. "We had expectations of learning about more men held in Laos."

The Pentagon was particularly concerned about fifty-three men who were definitely considered to be held in Laos. Pentagon sources at that time said some of these fifty-three were "known" to be held in Laos. None of these prisoners were included on the ten-man list turned over in Paris.

By early February, both the State Department and the Pentagon were certain that many more men than acknowledged were held in Laos. The air force, perhaps to demonstrate U.S. determination, continued B-52 bombing of remote areas of Laos. The thinking was that, although the Paris accords ended such flights over North Vietnam, continuation of these missions just a few miles west of Vietnam sent a strong message to the leaders in Hanoi: Live within the terms of the just-signed agreement or the bombers will return to Vietnam.

On February 6, 1973, an EC 47Q, a highly sophisticated U.S. Air Force reconnaissance aircraft, was shot down in Laos with seven men on board. Three men perished in the crash. Four men managed to bail out and were subsequently captured by Vietnamese army soldiers in the vicinity of the crash site. Hours later, in the Pentagon, there was consternation. Were these men held by Hanoi, even though they were captured in Laos? Were they POWs covered under the terms of the Paris accords, even though Laos and the Pathet Lao were not signatories to that agreement and even though this plane was shot down after the signing of the Paris agreement?

What to do? Washington chose deceit. After a preliminary decision to declare all seven men killed in action (KIA), despite certain evidence to the contrary, Acting Defense Secretary William Clements ordered everyone to keep quiet about any men held alive in Laos. Only through the courageous action of one Pentagon official was this decision reversed, and the seven men were finally listed as missing in action (MIA).

While that debate continued quietly inside the Pentagon, the first group of thin POWs freed by Hanoi under the terms of the Paris accords appeared on U.S. television. Millions of Americans stayed up at night to witness the arrival of the first planeload of just-released prisoners as they deplaned at Clark Field in the Philippines. One by one they strode purposefully down the plane's unloading ramp, were met individually by a welcoming officer, and then saluted the U.S. flag. Then they thanked "President Nixon, for bringing us home." For perhaps the only time during the Vietnam War, the whole nation had something to cheer: some of our heroes were home at last.

Another group of heroic POWs, however, was not coming home. There were no cheers for these men. They were being held in Laos, not for propaganda purposes, but for ransom. These prisoners were being held by Vietnam to exchange for the economic aid promised in the Nixon letter. The American people and Congress, however, were never told of the Nixon letter. The American people would not be told of it for four more years, not until Jimmy Carter became president.

During February and March of 1973, Hanoi, under the terms of the Paris accords, was to release the 591 POWs they acknowledged holding in Vietnam. Hanoi could, of course, at any time, stop or delay the release of these men. Secretary of State William Rogers was dispatched by Nixon and National Security Advisor Henry Kissinger to Capitol Hill to urge members of Congress to mute their anger over the reports of torture and deprivation coming from the first group of released prisoners. Rogers asked for "restraint" in statements by congressmen and senators. There was time enough to tell the world about Vietnamese brutality after all American POWs had been released. Clearly, for the immediate future, the growing anger among the American people over the treatment of these POWs stopped any thought that Congress would appropriate billions to "heal the wounds of war" in Vietnam. The administration worried that Hanoi might then delay or even cancel the prisoner release if Congress declared against Vietnamese aid at this time.

Had this same Congress known of the secret quid pro quo linking the economic aid payments and the unreleased POWs in Laos, then, no doubt, Congress would have so acted in order to gain the freedom of these men. Congress might have begun by telling the American people about the linkage between the prisoners' freedom and the economic aid payments. The White House, however, never revealed the existence of this linkage. Secretary of State Rogers even denied the existence of any such pledge of funds. No such promise, said Rogers, was ever made to Hanoi.

Imagine the confusion at that time in Hanoi: the Vietnamese government held a letter from the president of the United States clearly pledging in excess of $4 billion, while the secretary of state denied any such pledge.

On February 19, 1973, a spokesman for the Pathet Lao based in Vientiane, Laos, made a public announcement on the American POWs held by the Pathet Lao. "If they were captured in Laos, they will be released in Laos," Soth Petrasy was quoted in *Pacific Stars and Stripes* (February 19, 1973). He went on to state that the Pathet Lao had a detailed accounting of the prisoners and where they were being held. Soth Petrasy made clear that the conditions for the release of these prisoners required negotiations between Laos and the United States. No such negotiations for living American POWs has ever been held. Not one American POW held in Laos has ever been released.

By March 1973, a majority of the 591 American POWs held by Hanoi in North Vietnam had been released according to schedule. Nothing had been done about the prisoners in Laos. The B-52 and F-111 bombing missions continued in Laos. Capitol Hill remained in an angry uproar over the stories of the treatment of the prisoners just now appearing on the morning and evening news. Congress was not going to appropriate $4.75 billion to pay Hanoi—not after it had become clear that Vietnam had routinely beaten and tortured American prisoners in order to extract false confessions and propaganda statements.

Henry Kissinger made one last secret attempt to secure the release of the prisoners in Laos. He quietly sent Major Robert ("Bud") McFarlane, one of his military aides, to Paris to offer a new deal to the North Vietnamese. If Hanoi would arrange the release of the POWs in Laos, President Nixon would immediately pay Hanoi, out of presidential discretionary funds, $100 million in the form of medical supplies for the city of Vinh. The Vietnamese, intrigued by the new offer, asked for a day to deliberate. The response a day later was a refusal. Hanoi would, in effect, wait for the full $4.75 billion Nixon had pledged in his February 1 letter. Again, no agreement was reached to return the American prisoners in Laos.

By the end of March, the domestic political debacle, now known as Watergate, was on the president's horizon. Judge John Sirica was becoming a household name as the trial of the Watergate burglars began to dominate the news. Names like John Dean, Bob Haldemann, and John Ehrlichman replaced Danang, Saigon, and Hanoi on the evening news. The American people, exhausted by years of an Asian war, now turned their attention to a developing Constitutional crisis in Washington.

At about this time, the Pentagon began to lose hope about the American POWs still held in Laos. U.S. officials told the press they feared that this group of Americans would be used as pawns in the difficult dealings between Washington and Hanoi. These pawns were stuck between the two nations. Hanoi was using them as an insurance policy to guarantee the payment of the $4.75 billion that had been privately pledged but publicly denied. Washington, on the other hand, was scrambling to keep the private pledge private and, at the same time, to secure the release of these POWs. Ultimately, both sides lost. Hanoi never received a dollar of the promised U.S. aid, and not one man held in the Pathet Lao POW system has ever been released.

## III

From April 1973 until August 1974, when Nixon resigned the presidency, Watergate consumed the political energies of the United States. Media coverage of this scandal was unprecedented in scope and intensity. It was as if the nation, so bitter and discouraged over its defeat in Vietnam, turned all its disappointment into the destruction of one of the war's major players, Richard Nixon. Given this scandal, this crisis, this spectacle, Americans lost interest in Vietnam and the Paris peace agreement.

As Gerald Ford assumed the presidency in the East Room of the White House on that muggy August morning, Hanoi's military forces were steadily gaining on the battlefield in South Vietnam. The fears of North Vietnam's leaders that Washington would use military force to enforce the Paris agreements had been allayed by the increasing impotence of President Nixon. The message to Hanoi became clear: Americans no longer care about the destruction of South Vietnam.

Indeed, the only issue left from the Vietnam War that could still arouse any public attention was the haunting belief that some American POWs were still being held captive by Hanoi. Gerald Ford, keeping the Nixon foreign policy team, was the pupil; Henry Kissinger, now secretary of state, was the tutor. Kissinger, in a tantrum over Hanoi's alleged violations of the Paris accords, declared that the treaty was no longer applicable. He especially denied that the United States government had ever made a "firm commitment" to give any aid, economic or otherwise, to Hanoi.

Amid this confusion over the applicability of the Paris agreement, the House of Representatives attempted to answer the many questions about the remaining POWs. A special committee, headed by Mississippi Democrat Gillespie ("Sonny") Montgomery, was commissioned. During the investigation, the committee questioned high-level administration officials, journeyed to Vietnam, and even spoke to former president Nixon about the alleged promises of economic assistance made to Hanoi.

This House committee, however, was no match for Kissinger and company. The arrogance, perfidy, and dishonesty of the latter is easily seen. First, Kissinger refused to testify before this committee under oath. Next, he would agree only to an informal breakfast meeting. Thus, before traveling to Hanoi, the committee called one of Kissinger's most trusted assistants, Philip Habib, under secretary of state. Habib, during his testimony, was asked time and again if there existed any secret letters, understandings, or special arrangements. The House committee wanted exact answers. Did Kissinger and company have any information to help them? Habib assured the members of the committee that he could not help them.

The Vietnamese foreign ministry, however, did help. In Hanoi, the Vietnamese produced a copy of the February 1, 1973, Nixon letter that pledged between $3.25 billion and $4.75 billion.

Upon returning to Washington, the now-irate committee recalled Habib. Why had he not disclosed the existence of the Nixon letter? Habib quickly shifted his story. He claimed that he did not know of the existence of the letter. Furthermore, he said, "I can assure," said Habib, "that it [the letter] was not a commitment." (See Appendix B.)

Congressman Henry Gonzalez summarized the confusion and anger of his colleagues: "I believe it is demeaning to find Members of the U.S. House of Representatives confronting an erstwhile enemy just as bitter now as he was during the actual warfare, to be told something that was denied them by their own leaders of our country." (See Appendix B.)

This was not the first instance of congressional confusion and anger. Throughout the Vietnam War, not only had Congress been deceived, but also the American people had been asked to believe much that was not true. Yet no other administration falsehood was more reprehensible and none had a more tragic result. Because Kissinger and Habib refused to admit that the United States had reneged on a firm, presidential commitment to give "reconstruction" money to North Vietnam, the American POWs, now being held as insurance policies and negotiating instruments, were not released.

Congress, specifically the Montgomery committee, was not told of the extent of administration negotiations for the POWs remaining in Vietnam. The secret McFarlane mission of March 1973 was not described to Congress until nine years later, in 1982. Even then, even after admitting that he had gone to Paris on such a mission, McFarlane tried to deny it. The Nixon letter offering the money to Vietnam was never shown to anyone outside the executive branch until the Carter administration took office in 1977. Thus, Congressmnan Montgomery was ill prepared and ill informed when he concluded that there were "no Americans still being held alive as prisoners in Indochina, or elsewhere, as a result of the war in Indochina."

The Montgomery committee used, in part, the words of Vietnamese officials. They had denied repeatedly even violating the letter and spirit of the Paris accords. Hanoi, however, had always acted cleverly in constructing treaty language. The Paris Peace Accords did not cover Laos, did not cover any men held in Laos, and did not cover any men held in Laos even if they were held by the North Vietnamese. The Paris Peace Accords covered only 591 men. These 591 men had been returned to the United States in February and March 1973.

After returning these men, why would Hanoi deny having other American POWs? To answer this question, Hanoi's wartime strategy must be recalled. During the war the North Vietnamese were successful, in part, because they formed an informal public relations alliance with the American people. Hanoi joined the American people in the battle against the government in Washington. With the war over, Hanoi saw no reason to change this strategy in order to win the peace. Hanoi decided to continue this policy—this alliance with the American people—in the battle to secure the much-needed reconstruction money to "heal the wounds of war." To openly admit to holding American prisoners would alienate the American people and would break the alliance with them. Thus, Hanoi constructed a standard diplomatic dodge claiming that there may be prisoners in Laos, and, if so, Hanoi has nothing to do with them. Hanoi would, however, in the spirit of peace, justice, and reconciliation, intercede with the sovereign state of Laos to secure the release of these POWs. Until Washington produced the previously promised economic aid, Hanoi could refuse to intercede with Laos to recover the prisoners.

If Congress had been told about Nixon's letter and about the POWs in Laos, the American people would have demanded that negotiations be conducted to bring them home. Kissinger knew that they would not have settled for less. Hence, for Kissinger, the truth of the affair could not come out. He either kept important items from Philip Habib, his under secretary, or Kissinger ordered Habib to perjure himself before Congress. Next, Kissinger invoked executive privilege to prevent the release of the Nixon letter, even after Nixon had left office. Then, to deflect questions away from himself, Kissinger repeatedly refused to testify under oath about these matters.

For Kissinger, the truth could not come out because he could not accept the obvious conclusion that Hanoi had outnegotiated him. Hanoi had won the war, and the major battle forcing the United States to withdraw had been, in fact, fought in Paris. Without Kissinger's Paris Peace Accords, Hanoi could not have won. Now, in 1975, Kissinger could not afford to be outnegotiated again with the reparations promised in Nixon's letter and with the recovery of POWs actually held back for this specific eventuality. He had won the Nobel Peace Prize for his work in ending the Vietnam War; if he had told the truth about the POWs, Kissinger's failure would produce public humiliation. Kissinger was not going to look like a fool, he was not going to return his prize, and he was not going to tell the truth.

By 1976, when the Nixon, Ford, and Kissinger team was replaced by Jimmy Carter, Hanoi had realized its dream of total control over all of Vietnam. Hanoi, however, had failed to win from Washington the much-needed economic assistance so necessary to reconstruct their war-shattered country. Kissinger left office with a million-dollar advance to write his memoirs and with a reputation as a skillful negotiator. Congress adjourned with a new official finding that no POWs were held alive in Indochina.

In 1976, over four hundred American prisoners of war languished in despair in Southeast Asia. These men had to wonder what happened in Washington. Who in their government forced them to spend years of their lives in captivity? How many more years would they spend repairing abandoned U.S. military equipment? Did these men know that they had become pawns in the diplomatic struggle between Hanoi and Washington?

## IV

After Jimmy Carter was sworn in as the nation's thirty-ninth president, he was denied the Kissinger team's knowledge of the previous eight years of dealing with Hanoi. Almost all of the information about those dealings left with Kissinger; he had not involved the foreign service professionals and had not left much of a paper record. Only a handful of Kissinger's National Security Council (NSC) team were aware of the truth about secret arrangements with Hanoi. Only Kissinger himself knew the whole story. When he left office in January 1977, almost all the institutional knowledge of the remaining POWs in Indochina also left. The truth about the Nixon letter was not told to Jimmy Carter.

Jimmy Carter's manner, however, was different. He wanted to bring an openness to the Oval Office. He also brought an ignorance and naiveté perhaps never seen before in the White House. In one of his first interviews after his inauguration, the new president admitted to *Time* magazine that he could not name the leaders of most of the countries in the Middle East. Nevertheless, Carter was not unaware of public relations in the post-Watergate era. Carter had known during his recent campaign that he had to be the exact opposite of Nixon. Now, as president, Jimmy Carter decided to follow the same axiom. For example, President Carter set about to perform a diplomatic triple-header: he wanted the normalization of relations with China, Vietnam, and Cuba.

With Vietnam, the outstanding issue that prevented normalizing relations was the resolution of the POW/MIA issue. Carter needed a quick, cosmetic way to finesse that obstacle; he would find a way to reclassify the POWs and MIAs as KIAs (killed in action, body not recovered). Shortly after his inauguration, he found the exact solution. Carter was able to kill two birds with one stone by rewarding a major political supporter, Leonard Woodcock, the former leader of the United Auto Workers of America (UAW), with the appointment to head a special panel that would report to the president on the MIA issue. The chairman of the recently dissolved House committee on this issue, Congressman Sonny Montgomery, was appointed to the Woodcock panel, as was former Senator Mike Mansfield who, like Woodcock, was angling for a substantial political appointment.

Without doing any background work or employing any professional intelligence officers, the Woodcock panel made their one and only trip to Southeast Asia from March 16 to 19, 1977. While in Hanoi, Woodcock was assured that the Vietnamese were doing everything possible to locate the remains of U.S. servicemen. Nevertheless, on the subject of living Americans, Hanoi was evasive. Hanoi merely said that "no Americans who registered with Hanoi remain in Vietnam." Further, the Vietnamese officials refused to elaborate on cases of Americans who might have refused to "register" or exactly what constituted "registration."

Woodcock and company, satisfied with this boiler-plate denial, rushed back to Washington. Woodcock, after his first diplomatic foray, recommended that the president believe the Vietnamese. Carter admitted to no experience and little working knowledge of Southeast Asia. He knew nothing of the intricacies of the Vietnam War or the Paris Peace Accords. Above all, Carter knew absolutely nothing, thanks to Henry Kissinger, about the secret agreements between Washington and Hanoi.

Leonard Woodcock, with perhaps even less foreign policy background than Carter, but having delivered the UAW endorsement to the then-unknown Georgian, was named, in return for his non-confrontational and noncontroversial commission assignment, special representative to Beijing. Mike Mansfield was named ambassador to Japan. Sonny Montgomery, the point man from the House on the POW/MIA issue, was spared the embarrassment of admitting that he and his committee had been wrong. Montgomery rubber-stamped the results of the Woodcock commission.

The Woodcock commission became a self-fulfilling prophecy. Knowing that Carter had already decided to normalize relations with Vietnam, Hanoi's leaders had no need to use the POWs as bait. Why dangle something in Carter's face when Carter was about to jump in the net anyway?

As a result of the commission's report and recommendations, President Jimmy Carter ordered the reclassification of the POWs and MIAs. Over the final months of 1977 and most of 1978, the Pentagon proceeded to reclassify most men as killed in action, body not recovered. The POW/MIA families complained bitterly. They all felt that the president had given away what little leverage they had on Hanoi and that he was telling them to even give up any hope of the men returning.

Congressman Benjamin Gilman, a member of the Montgomery committee, criticized the Woodcock commission for not preparing properly and for being too hasty in finishing its work. Gilman said that Woodcock and company had "compounded the felony" of the Montgomery committee, which was not justified in coming to the conclusion that there were no POWs still held in Southeast Asia.

With the POW/MIA issue no longer in existence, the way was cleared to normalize relations with Hanoi in the fall of 1978. However, bureaucratic infighting between the State Department and the Pentagon, combined with newfound political vulnerability in the Carter White House in the summer and fall of 1978, caused the hoped-for diplomatic triple-header to be reduced to the single act of recognition of China in December 1978. Learning in October 1978 that once again Washington had shunned them, Hanoi's leaders turned to Moscow for economic aid. The price for this aid was not a surprise: the Soviets demanded an increased political and military role in the region, especially bases for Soviet soldiers and sailors. In addition, with a Soviet prod and a push, Vietnam invaded Kampuchea in late December 1978, less than two weeks after Washington's recognition of Beijing.

Vietnamese officials today are adamant about one point: had Carter proceeded with his plans to normalize relations with Hanoi,

Vietnam would not have invaded Kampuchea and would not have rushed into the arms of the Soviets. Improved relations and trade with the West, particularly the United States, was then and remains today Hanoi's goal. Vietnam would not have forsaken that goal by invading Kampuchea. Once Washington shunned Hanoi, however, and moved closer to Hanoi's historic adversary, China, the Vietnamese were forced—or, as one Hanoi official recently put it, "bent at the elbow"—to move toward Moscow.

The result, of course, proved unsatisfactory for everyone, except the Soviets. Vietnam's economy virtually disintegrated. The continued presence of the Vietnamese army in Kampuchea caused them to become an international pariah. China grew increasingly hostile to Vietnam, withdrawing most of its support in 1978. The United States became a minor player in the region. The American prisoners of war languished.

Jimmy Carter diminished in power and prestige. By 1979, he faced severe domestic political difficulties, especially in his own party. His administration paid no more attention to Vietnam or the POW issue after the Kampuchean situation, other than to join the international chorus in condemning Hanoi's actions. Instead, Carter's focus was on the Middle East, first with the Camp David Accords and then with the Iranian hostage situation. For his final year in the White House, Carter was consumed with securing the release of Americans held against their will. Carter, unfortunately, labored to free only the fifty-three held by Iran, not also the hundreds still held by the Communist forces in Southeast Asia.

## V

The election of Ronald Reagan, surprisingly, did not result in a renewed focus on the POW issues. Governor Reagan of California had been one of the most vocal supporters of the issue. When the 591 POWs returned in early 1973, Governor Reagan made a point of greeting as many of them as possible, since many of them were from California or had been based there. In his first year in the Oval Office, President Reagan looked back fondly on that homecoming, "I remember staying up all night to see those men land at Clark Field in the Philippines. And how they walked down the ramp, saluted the flag and then thanked us for bringing them home." Reagan finished this anecdote with emotion, as if on the verge of tears. If ever there was a president who would try to bring home the remaining POWs, it would be Reagan. If the price for that repatriation required improving relations with the government in Hanoi, then Reagan was well-suited politically for that task. If anti–Communist Richard Nixon could go to China, then anti–Communist Ronald Reagan could recognize Vietnam.

The surprise was that President Reagan's administration did not reflect his genuine concern for the POWs. Of the five administrations in office since the POWs became an issue, Johnson's, Nixon's, Ford's, Carter's, and Reagan's, the Reagan administration did the least. The public rhetoric, as with many issues, was imaginative and satisfying, but the follow-up was ineffectual and often contrary to the public pronouncements. In fact, the deception in the POW issue that had begun under Kissinger increased under Reagan and his several national security advisors. For example, after much prodding from members of his own party in the House of Representatives, President Reagan declared the POW issue to be "the highest national priority of this administration." But in spite of this declaration, Jeane Kirkpatrick, while she was a member of the Reagan cabinet as ambassador to the United Nations, was able to say to me in 1985, "I never once attended any White House meeting where the subject was ever mentioned."

Another example: National Security Advisor Robert McFarlane, who had undertaken in 1973 a secret mission for Kissinger in a desperate attempt to recover left-behind POWs, admitted in 1985 that, despite the rhetoric, "we haven't even begun to start to solve the problem. We have no on-the-ground human intelligence in the region." He also conceded that American POWs were still being held alive in Southeast Asia. "They must be there," he told a group of businessmen at an Evans-Novak Forum in Washington, D.C.

The POW issue, having been declared as the highest national priority, was given to a lieutenant colonel on the National Security Council staff. A lieutenant colonel was asked to run an issue with the highest national priority! The State Department's senior political appointees were totally removed from all analysis and decision making on the issue. Deputy Secretary of State John C. Whitehead repeatedly attempted to have operational authority for this diplomatic issue transferred to his department. Every national security advisor from John Poindexter to Frank Carlucci to Colin Powell refused Whitehead's request. In the State Department, Under Secretary of State Edward Derwinski admitted that he and his office were not informed or consulted about formulation of policy toward Vietnam or the POW/MIA Issue.

From outside the administration, former senator John Tower, appointed by President Reagan in the wake of the Iran/contra scandal to investigate the National Security Council, specifically examined the handling of the POW issue by the NSC staff. Senator Tower, declaring that the staff of the NSC should not be an operational staff, strongly urged National Security Advisor Frank Carlucci to move the jurisdiction of this issue over to Secretary Whitehead at the State department. It is no surprise that Carlucci refused.

## VI

During the Reagan administration, the POW issue became an excuse not to improve relations between Washington and Hanoi, instead of a reason to draw closer together. The Reagan White House consistently rejected attempts by Vietnam to settle the POW issue in return for diplomatic recognition and economic assistance. In each instance, these offers were rejected out of hand.

Some Washington sources, for example, reported that within two weeks of Reagan's first inauguration, Hanoi offered to return fifty-three Americans to the United States for $4 billion in aid. The offer was allegedly transmitted through Canada, and it may have actually been made during the transition period, so as to offer outgoing President Carter the opportunity to bring fifty-three Americans home from Southeast Asia while he was failing to bring fifty-three other Americans home from Iran.

This Vietnamese offer allegedly was on the agenda of a meeting of the president, senior White House aides Edwin Meese and Michael Deaver, Central Intelligence Agency (CIA) Director William Casey, and National Security Advisor Richard Allen. According to sources in the meeting, a senior staffer was vehement in opposing any payments to Hanoi. His opposition reflected the recently concluded Iranian hostage crisis. One presidency had just been destroyed by Americans held hostage. The new president was now being asked to pay a ransom to Vietnam. The last thing Reagan needed at the time was the attention of the American people drawn back to the horrors and failures of the last fifteen years in Indochina. The new administration first had to gear up a much-needed economic recovery program.

Only Richard Allen raised strong objections. He argued that these American POWs ought to be brought home. Reagan agreed. In typical Reaganesque manner, he left the details to be handled by his staff, directing them to "try to find another way to handle this."

The staff did find another way to handle the POW issue. Orders went out to stall, to delay, and to downplay this potentially explosive issue. Thus, when, as a congressman, I and another congressman reached an agreement with the Hanoi-controlled government of Laos, the Reagan staff quickly aborted the arrangement, undoubtedly out of fear that it could lead to recovery of American prisoners of war.

The agreement made with Vientiane was that in exchange for $200,000 in medical supplies from the U.S. Agency for International Development (AID), the Laotians would, for the very first time, officially order local officials to ask, in the words of their deputy foreign minister, "their people and farmers to search for American MIAs." Of course, for the Laotians, the Americans remaining in Laos were not prisoners. These Americans were war criminals or volunteers who remained behind to heal the wounds of war. These words, *criminal* and *volunteer,* were just devices to help the Communists to save face. The reality is that they wanted, and still want, to trade American POWs for American economic assistance.

By February 1982, when this agreement with the Laotians needed nurturing by the administration, the recently installed deputy national security advisor was Robert McFarlane, Kissinger's military aide in 1973. Following the stall and delay plan, McFarlane refused to allow any more medical shipments to Laos. No explanation was given. Because of this order, the Laotian government reversed course and stopped searching for American MIAs.

Similarly, in another instance of the White House desire to stall, delay, and downplay, the Pentagon's Defense Intelligence Agency

(DIA), chartered to be the lead agency with the POW/MIA issue, ran a series of on-the-ground human intelligence missions into Laos to determine if a newly constructed detention center near Kham Keut contained American prisoners. Although the results of these missions are classified, much of the information gathered indicated that American POWs were being held there. Again, the Reagan administration stepped in to downplay the significance of these intelligence missions.

The administration even went so far in the early spring of 1982 to prepare a contingency plan in the eventuality that some American POWs would be recovered by a private group or simply released by forces inside Laos. In late March 1982, Assistant Secretary of Defense Richard Armitage called an off-the-record Pentagon press briefing. His purpose? He wanted to plant the seed, without attribution, that if any Americans were still in Laos, they were either defectors or drug addicts. In addition, the U.S. ambassador to Thailand, John Gunther Dean, was ordered to follow Armitage's off-the-record line. The intent? Armitage and Dean wanted to discredit in advance any Americans coming out of Southeast Asia, so as to minimize the media impact of their return.

Despite these repeated attempts by the Reagan administration to stall, delay, and downplay the POW issue, the years from 1982 to 1988 saw a media and public explosion of interest in the U.S. soldiers, sailors, and airmen remaining in Southeast Asia. Instead of a decrease in interest, which would naturally occur as time went on and as Vietnam became a distant, unpleasant memory, the POW issue has grown into a major national concern. The Reagan White House pollster, Richard Wirthlin, was surprised by the results of a national survey he conducted in June 1987. An overwhelming 82 percent of the American public believed that "there are American POWs being held against their will in Vietnam and Laos." Furthermore, 71 percent did not believe that "the Reagan Administration was doing all it could to recover these men." Over 50 percent believed there is "a cover-up of the truth about the POWs in Washington."

Thus, despite White House attempts to ignore or cosmetically handle the POW issue, the American people, as seen from Wirthlin's national survey, were not fooled. Nevertheless, the Reagan administration clung to the position, adopted in 1981, that "while we can't preclude the possibility that Americans may be held against their will, we have no evidence to prove it."

This White House position, moreover, was contradicted by other administration figures. The Pentagon, for example, appointed a special blue-ribbon panel to look into the DIA's handling of this issue. Chaired by a former director of the DIA, General Eugene Tighe, this commission returned after five months of study to say they believed that "Americans are being held in Southeast Asia." Tighe himself is much more adamant. He is certain there are American POWs being held. Tighe cannot understand why there is so much resistance to changing U.S. policy toward Hanoi in order to settle this issue. He has said, "I continue to encounter a civilian mind-set to debunk any report of POW's held against their will."

McFarlane also contradicted this White House position when he, perhaps wracked by a guilty conscience, admitted in 1985 that there were American prisoners held in Southeast Asia. At the same time, McFarlane said, "We haven't even begun to start to solve this problem."

Central to a solution of this problem has been a key question: should U.S. policy on Vietnam be changed? As a result of the critique by the Reagan Right, the White House took yet another cosmetic step in 1987. General John Vessey was appointed a special presidential envoy to Hanoi. However, unknown to the public, General Vessey was told by the White House not to discuss the normalization of relations with Hanoi and not to link U.S. economic assistance to Vietnam to a settlement of the POW issue. For the White House, Vessey was to appear to be addressing the issue; in reality he was following the stall-delay-downplay policy set by the White House staff in 1981.

Hanoi was disappointed. The new leaders in Vietnam hoped a presidential envoy would be carrying instructions about their first concern, an American offer of diplomatic normalization. Instead, all Vessey could produce for Vietnam was a nebulous proposal to have private U.S. charities (nongovernmental organizations) deliver a few prosthetic devices for the war wounded.

Once again, Washington took the position that there could be no normalization of relations until the POW issue was totally settled. Hanoi, in turn, stuck to its position that in order to settle the

POW issue, Hanoi must first receive economic help from the United States.

In early 1988, Vietnamese Foreign Minister Nguyen Co Thach officially rejected this so-called Vessey Initiative. He said to a group of visiting journalists, "My people will ask why the United States refuses to give government aid to Vietnam while Vietnam gives government aid to the United States." Thach was referring to Vietnamese searches for Americans unaccounted for after the war. The foreign minister added, "We believe the establishment of relations should not wait but should be as soon as possible." Once again, the POW issue and U.S. economic assistance to Hanoi were directly linked, as they were during and after the Paris Peace Accords in 1973.

## VII

The hard-line anti-Communists who dominated decision making inside the Reagan administration used the POW issue as a means not to improve relations with Hanoi. Washington should have realized long ago that working with—not against—Hanoi was the optimal solution for the POW/MIA problem. Only if Hanoi has an incentive to "find" the POWs will the United States ever see a final settlement.

To break the stalemate between Hanoi and Washington on the POW issue, the United States must take the first step. Normalizing relations does not mean a granting of approval of another nation's economic and political system. It does not mean the approval of a particular regime. The normalizing of relations is merely the acknowledgment of the other government's unquestioned rule of that nation. After relations have been normalized, the United States can continue to disagree with and criticize Hanoi, all the while attempting to engage the Vietnamese leadership in negotiations on all issues. Indeed, Hanoi desperately seeks U.S. diplomatic recognition because it represents a stamp of legitimacy, ultimately leading to trade with the West and loans from the World Bank, the International Monetary Fund (IMF), and the Asian Development Bank. In taking the first step, the immediate normalization of relations with Hanoi, ambassadors should be exchanged and embassies set up with absolutely no quid pro quo expected or given on any issue. This first step will allow both the United States and Vietnam to enter the full community of nations.

With this first move, Americans should not delude themselves: Hanoi will continue to use all levers, especially the POW/MIA issue to obtain what it needs from Washington. After Vietnam has been recognized officially by Washington, Vietnamese behavior will not immediately change. The wooing of Hanoi will have begun, and Hanoi is more than willing to work with Americans and more than ready to move away from the Soviets.

As a second step, the United States should publicly announce a timetable and schedule of those events leading to (1) the granting of most favored nation trading status, (2) the lifting of the trade embargo, (3) the making of recommendations to the IMF and World Bank for loans to Hanoi, and (4) the granting of some large-scale medical assistance to Vietnam. All these moves should be made contingent on substantial progress on the recovery of living American prisoners. The remains alone are of little national interest until the living prisoners are repatriated.

To this end, as a third step, the United States should make one unilateral concession to the Indochinese Communists: the Vietnamese and Americans must construct a way for the Communists to save face as they return the living Americans they have for so long denied holding. One solution, for example, is to agree that the American prisoners have not been held by the current regime in Hanoi, but, instead, have been found by Hanoi. In a similar vein, both countries could agree that these American POWs have been held in Laos, not a signatory to the Paris Peace Accords. Hanoi, the story would be, used its good offices with Vientiane to assure the release of these men.

There are a number of precedents for a face-saving arrangement. In the case of the capture, for example, of the U.S.S. Pueblo in 1968, the United States agreed to sign a completely false statement, which contained an admission by the United States that the Pueblo had violated the sovereign territory of North Korea. Immediately after signing, a precondition for the return of the crew, the U.S. negotiator told the international press corps that the signed statement was false. The crew of the Pueblo, however, was released, and North Korea felt vindicated by the U.S. signature. Both sides were satisfied.

Both Hanoi and Washington, similarly, need to be satisfied with any settlement of the POW issue. A face-saving mechanism must be central to any agreement.

Once the first steps have been taken, then the broader, regional political motivations for improved relations between Hanoi and Washington will tempt Hanoi to turn away from Moscow and into a position to play the two superpowers and China off each other. It will be U.S. trade and technology, nevertheless, which will ultimately draw Vietnam closer to the United States. Influenced especially by the economic development of the other Southeast Asian nations, the leaders of Vietnam see that only with technological development—immediate technological development—will their nation survive.

The American prisoners of war serve only one purpose for Hanoi. They are the bait to attract the United States. Once that task is accomplished, Vietnam can be induced to help bring about the return of the American prisoners. Only Washington can begin the new relationship with Hanoi; only Washington can bring Hanoi back into the international community. And, strange to say, only Washington can ensure the long-term well-being of Vietnam.

For Americans, no political analysis, geopolitical or psychological, will explain or erase the crime of holding the prisoners. The Communists held the American prisoners. Washington abandoned them. Both sides lied to the American people about these men. Will all the pain of the many days, months, and years of suffering by these men be made to mean something if their return brings about a new understanding between the two former adversaries?

# 5

# WHO MAKES THE POLICY?
# A CANCER ON THE
# EXECUTIVE BRANCH

## I

It is clear that the United States government has adopted a hard-line policy toward Vietnam. Included in that policy are the two conditions of a Hanoi troop pullout from Kampuchea and a full accounting of U.S. soldiers missing from the war prior to the normalization of relations. In itself, this policy is not abnormal, especially for a conservative, hard-line administration such as the Reagan administration. However, what is odd is the way the policy was conceived—and who conceived it. Did President Reagan involve himself in the formulation of this policy? Did Secretary of State Shultz run what is basically a diplomatic issue? Which executive branch department took the lead in the formulation of this policy? Which department carried out the policy? Was there a healthy internal debate within the administration over this policy? Was dissent welcome?

In the summer and fall of 1987, a select joint Senate-House panel concluded that "a secret foreign policy" had been adopted and implemented in the Iran/contra affair. The committee found that the normal National Security Council process of setting policy had been subverted by a handful of NSC staffers, perhaps with the concurrence of President Reagan. Is it possible that a similar subversion of the NSC process could have occurred in the case of setting policy with Vietnam? Could there also be a secret foreign policy for Vietnam?

On July 7, 1987, President Reagan explained the process of making foreign policy toward Vietnam to Anthony D. Duke in a private letter: "The effort is government-wide and does not rest in any one agency due to the complexity of the issue. The Department of State chairs the interagency group, which includes all agencies, while the Department of Defense acts as Executive Agent. The NSC staff participates in all meetings and provides active oversight for me. This process has served us well."

The interagency group, known as the IAG, has been chaired by Deputy Assistant Secretary of State for Pacific Affairs David Lambertson. On all matters concerning Vietnam, Lambertson and his IAG set forth the policy. This is curious in light of the president's oft-repeated statement that the solution to the POW/MIA issue, the single largest bilateral issue between Washington and Hanoi, was his administration's "highest national priority." Yet, if it was truly the "highest national priority," why was only a deputy assistant secretary of state handling it?

Despite the president's letter outlining the policy mechanism of his administration, others found contrary evidence. For example, from 1982 to 1987, the IAG met infrequently, no formal records of the meetings or their agendas were kept, the State Department was cut out of policy making, and all overseas trips and negotiations were handled by one United States Army lieutenant colonel on the National Security Council staff. Indeed, the tale of this lieutenant colonel is amazingly similar to that of another now famous military officer serving on the National Security Council staff.

During the height of the congressional debate of the sale of the AWACS planes to Saudi Arabia in the summer of 1981, National Security Advisor Richard Allen requested some additional staff support from the Pentagon. Two junior officers were temporarily detailed to Allen's office, supposedly for simple tasks such as chart turning during Senate briefings. These two officers, one a marine and the other from the army, were placed in the NSC's Office of Politico-Military Affairs. Both officers remained well past their "temporary" assignment and survived the firings, resignations, and transfers of Allen, Judge William Clark, and Robert McFarlane. Both officers soon were doing much more than flipping charts. Each traveled extensively to conduct negotiations with foreign governments. Each wielded enormous power inside Washington, acting with carte blanche to speak on behalf of the president, to brief the press, to meet with citizens, and to brief members of Congress.

Both of these military officers also participated in domestic political affairs to the extent that they raised money for projects and uttered their views of certain congressmen and senators, thereby indicating their preferences in upcoming elections. Each also claimed to have a close personal relationship with President Reagan.

The more famous of these two junior officers is Lt. Col. Oliver North, who rose to international prominence during the unraveling of the Iran/contra scandal. His activities are now known to all. However, the other officer who came to the White House "temporarily" in 1981, Lt. Col. Richard Childress, survived even longer than did North. Childress stayed on after Poindexter and North were removed. He became director of the Asian Desk at the National Security Staff, as the Office of Politico-Military Affairs was abolished. (North and Childress were both directors of this desk.) He survived the appointment of Frank Carlucci, who tried to clean house at the NSC. Childress also remained after Carlucci left to be replaced as national security advisor by General Colin Powell.

In his almost seven years as an NSC staffer, Richard Childress, supposedly a former artillery officer, personally handled almost all negotiations with the governments of Vietnam and Laos. Contrary to President Reagan's letter, the NSC staff did much more than just keep an eye on things for the president. In fact, the NSC staff was running all relations with these foreign governments in complete controversion of the normal procedures for formulating policy.

In the wake of Iran/contra revelations, President Reagan tasked former senator John Tower to look into the entire NSC system. Tower's written report did not contain his views of the handling of the Vietnam and POW issues, but he spent considerable time investigating those matters. His conclusion was that the National Security Council staff, in particular Richard Childress, had far exceeded their bounds in the conduct of policy. Tower immediately recommended that the operational authority for these primarily diplomatic issues be transferred over to the State Department. Frank Carlucci refused to relinquish NSC control. In fact, despite Tower's rebuke, Carlucci further authorized Childress to repeatedly travel to Vietnam and Laos. This, despite the Tower commission report stating that NSC staffers should not travel, should not negotiate with foreign governments, should be on the staff no longer than three years (if they were military officers detailed to the NSC), and should not brief the press.

The Tower board's chief-of-staff, Rhett Dawson, joined Howard Baker's White House staff and privately admitted in 1987 that Ollie North's original 1981 assignment to the NSC staff had been undercover. The chart-flipping was a cover for North's real purpose: he was a CIA agent hidden in uniform to run secret operations out of the NSC. In such a position, neither North nor North's projects required congressional oversight. Robert McFarlane confirmed this during the Iran/contra hearings, when he admitted that North actually reported to CIA Director William Casey, not to McFarlane, his nominal boss at the NSC. Former treasury secretary William Simon, a close friend of Casey, admitted to me in 1985, a year before the Iran/contra revelations, that "Ollie North wears a Marine uniform but he's actually a CIA man hidden inside the NSC." Rhett Dawson did not know if Childress was also an agent undercover.

Carlucci and his successor, Powell, ignored all of Tower's recommendations. They allowed Childress, an army officer, to stay seven years, not three. They continued to allow him to brief the press; in one briefing of the Associated Press, Childress labeled the families of POWs in Southeast Asia "crazies." Carlucci and Powell also continued to authorize Childress to conduct negotiations—all after the Tower report.

Only after the press began to inquire about the applicability of the Tower report to the conduct of policy making with regard to Vietnam did the National Security Council staff construct the above-mentioned new catch-all presidential statement intended to appear as if all the major departments were involved in policy making. In fact, nothing has changed: the NSC staff, not the State Department, makes and carries out policy.

For example, Deputy Secretary of State John C. Whitehead repeatedly tried to convince each National Security Advisor from Poindexter to Powell to transfer authority for the POW and Vietnam issues to the State Department, where he was prepared to bring in specialized personnel to work solely on these matters. Each time the NSC refused. Whitehead finally admitted in private that he had no power in formulating policy toward Vietnam; he was merely informed of the policy after that policy had already been implemented. When I asked him who in the administration made policy on Vietnam, Deputy Secretary Whitehead furrowed his brow and replied, "I don't know."

Similarly, Under Secretary of State Edward Derwinski, a Washington veteran, admitted that he was kept in the dark about all issues pertaining to Vietnam. He was not consulted. He was not invited to meetings. He was not informed of policy changes. On one occasion, the appointment of Special Presidential Envoy John Vessey, Derwinski first learned of it by reading about it in the *Washington Post*.

As mentioned earlier, another example of how rhetoric and reality differ on issues relating to Vietnam in the Reagan administration was seen when the U.S. ambassador to the United Nations, Jeane Kirkpatrick, admitted that despite the president's contention that the POW issue was his "highest national priority," she had never once heard the topic discussed during any cabinet, National Security Council, or State Department meeting.

If the deputy secretary of state, the under secretary of state, and the most influential U.N. ambassador in U.S. history all are cut out of policy making on issues pertaining to Vietnam, then who was running our government? If John Tower, charged with recommending reforms of the National Security Council and its staff, can be summarily ignored, who was truly in charge?


## II


In the summer of 1980, when it was clear that Ronald Reagan had successfully secured the Republican presidential nomination, his campaign manager, William Casey, set about assembling a first-class research team for the general election campaign against the incumbent president, Jimmy Carter. Casey drew upon a network of former Office of Strategic Services (OSS) and CIA employees, many of whom had retired during the late 1970s because of Carter's virtual decimation of the U.S. intelligence community. As a long-time booster of the need for intelligence, no matter the price, and because of a close relationship with the original head of the OSS,

Wild Bill Donovan, Casey enjoyed an excellent reputation among this close-knit but dispirited fraternity.

Casey was shrewd enough politically to know that Carter, despite the image as a pristine, religious man, was in fact a ruthless, tough campaigner who wouldn't hesitate to invoke any and all presidential authority in order to win the election. In particular, Casey feared an "October surprise" involving a sudden deal to release the fifty-three American hostages held in Iran by the forces loyal to the Ayatollah Khomeini. Casey's solution to this possibility was to put together a campaign intelligence team consisting of CIA and military intelligence alumni. For example, to warn of a possible surprise involving U.S. military personnel and equipment, Casey communicated with retired military personnel near all domestic military air bases. The hope was that any imminent air operation would be detected by these veterans through a change in flight traffic and patterns.

Casey also brought into the main Reagan campaign headquarters CIA veterans familiar with Iran. He demanded to learn everything he could about the Ayatollah, the Revolutionary Guards, and the hostage situation. During this process, Casey tapped into a new group of intelligence operatives, most of whom cut their teeth in Vietnam. They had been members of numerous projects in the secret war in Laos and operations such as the Phoenix Project in Vietnam.

Many of these same people were transferred to the Middle East following the fall of Saigon in 1975. And by late 1979 and early 1980, this group of now-hardened veterans of two disastrous U.S. defeats was ready to join in an effort to elect a new president devoted to strengthening the United States and reestablishing the nation as an assertive world leader. This group, in their late thirties and early forties by 1980, fit the profile of people Casey most respected: young, courageous, hungry, and bold. They were made in the image of Casey as he saw himself during World War II, when he served Donovan in London, running agents behind Nazi lines. Casey once remarked to me in 1980, somewhat wistfully, "I like my people to be lean and mean."

The October surprise never happened, and November brought a huge Reagan landslide and the appointment of William Casey to be the all-powerful Director of Central Intelligence (DCI). In this post, Casey oversaw not just the CIA, but also the National Security Agency, the Defense Intelligence Agency, the Intelligence Support Activity (ISA) inside the Pentagon, and other, secret intelligence outfits hidden throughout the government.

Casey's immediate task was to restore morale throughout the intelligence community. To do that, the new director used both his political clout and his personal clout with the First Family to place members of his "campaign team" throughout the executive branch. Some were hired back to work at the CIA, assured that the Reagan administration would not abandon them or "sell out," as the Ford and Carter administrations had. Casey, clever in his own right about the ways of Washington, placed some of his team on the staff of the National Security Council and inside the Pentagon hierarchy. In one celebrated bureaucratic battle, Casey succeeded in placing a CIA lawyer in a key Defense Department slot, before Defense Secretary Caspar Weinberger himself could fill that position. By the summer of 1981, the Casey team was in place. He could proceed to his next task: to pick a spot and roll back the advancing tide of communism.

## III

Ronald Reagan, William Casey, and Secretary of State Alexander Haig chose Central America as the battleground on which a new counteroffensive would be fought. All their attention and energy were focused on El Salvador and Nicaragua; Vietnam specifically and Southeast Asia in general were ignored, remembered as a recent bad memory and a domestic political negative. Thus, whenever a policy decision came to the White House regarding Vietnam, it was delegated downward into the administration's bureaucracy. Because it was a low priority, it was handled by a relatively low level official. As the American people learned during the Iran/contra hearings, Ronald Reagan's management style featured heavy reliance on staff and delegation of most decisions and all implementation.

Casey, about one year before he was stricken by a terminal brain tumor, confided to me in January 1986, "Reagan's got two faults. One is that he is the laziest man I've ever met. He never reads anything. And the second is that he allows his staff to undercut him." Casey, ever the loyalist, couldn't fathom how President Reagan could be tranquil in the face of White House staffers leaking information and manipulating the media in order to get the president to change his policies. It was these two traits—excessive delegation of major responsibilities and tolerating staffers with their own agendas—that initially led to a runaway NSC staff and almost total disarray in the foreign policy-making community. In the middle of all this, the Vietnam issue was allowed to be run, not as "the highest national priority," but rather as the private policy preserve of a group of hard-line appointees who, by themselves, determined and ran all policy toward Vietnam.

For example, John Sears, Ronald Reagan's campaign manager in 1976 and in 1980 before being replaced by Casey, recalls Casey bringing into the Reagan campaign, in the summer of 1980, a group of intelligence veterans to work in the general election. One of them was Richard Armitage, then in his midthirties, a navy and CIA veteran from the Vietnam War and Iran. After a brief fling as Robert Dole's administrative assistant, Armitage had been recruited and hired by Casey for the Reagan campaign.

Casey helped Armitage win appointment to the Pentagon post of deputy assistant secretary of defense for international security. Within months, Armitage was promoted to assistant secretary for international security, heading the Defense Department's "little State Department." With a loyalist in place in this crucial post, Casey firmly extended his reach throughout the executive branch.

Armitage, however, brought his own agenda to the job. As a CIA and military veteran, his views on Vietnam echoed other hardliners who wanted to continue the diplomatic and economic isolation of the Hanoi regime. Unencumbered by superiors interested in this issue, Armitage was virtually free to dominate all policy decisions regarding Vietnam. He assembled a team of friends and cronies, many of whom shared his intelligence background. For his principal deputy, he selected James Kelly, a long-time "company" man. (It was James Kelly's brother, John Kelly, another old CIA hand who, while serving as ambassador in Beirut, bypassed Secretary of State George Shultz and dealt directly with the NSC staff, including Oliver North and Robert McFarlane.) Another old friend, Gaston Sigur, ostensibly an expert on the Japanese economy, joined the National Security Council staff. General Richard Secord, another member of this group, was already serving as an assistant secretary of defense. Two other old agency friends, Ted Shackley and Tom Clines, were still operating on the periphery of the CIA. By late 1981 and early 1982, Richard Armitage, virtually unknown inside Washington, was the major policy maker on all issues having to do with Southeast Asia.

Normally, the State Department would be in conflict with Pentagon decisions, but curiously, in the Reagan administration these two competing departments have not disagreed on policy decisions regarding Vietnam. In the State Department, the lead official in the first Reagan term was Paul Wolfowitz as assistant secretary of state for Pacific and Asian affairs. He worked with Armitage, allowing the latter to set policy. Later, in the recurring game of musical chairs detailed below, Wolfowitz would be replaced by Sigur, who, in turn, was replaced at the NSC by Kelly.

William Casey and Ronald Reagan spent virtually no time on Vietnam or Southeast Asia. Neither had ever been there while in office or had any background or interest in the region. The vice-presidential national security advisor, Donald Gregg, however, was a long-time CIA veteran, having served as CIA station chief in Seoul and as deputy station chief in Saigon. He was also a long-time friend of Armitage.

When Judge William Clark replaced Richard Allen as the White House national security advisor in early 1982, he brought in, as his deputy, Robert McFarlane, who a decade before had served as Henry Kissinger's military aide and had carried out secret diplomatic trips in the wake of the collapsing Paris Peace Accords.

These three, Armitage, Gregg, and McFarlane, all veterans of the Vietnam debacle, dominated and determined all policy regarding Southeast Asia in general and Vietnam in particular. Because their superiors virtually abdicated their responsibility on these issues, these three men were allowed to speak for a president who had no desire to master the facts—and who was denied those facts in order to adopt policies clearly at odds with his public statements.

For example, the director of the Defense Intelligence Agency, Gen. Eugene Tighe, chartered to run the collection of information about the POW issue, was certain American POWs were being held against their will in 1982. He was not allowed to see President Reagan about this.

Similarly, two Republican congressmen (I was one of them) journeyed in early 1982 to Laos and secured a major policy breakthrough from the Pathet Lao government concerning efforts to "search" for living American prisoners out in the Laotian countryside. Yet, despite this and despite the fact that we were strong Reagan loyalists, McFarlane refused to allow us a meeting with President Reagan for three months. Only after Chief of Staff Jim Baker was threatened with severe political reprisals was a meeting scheduled. Even then, McFarlane continually interrupted the discussion in order to prevent the president from hearing the basic facts about the living American POWs held against their will.

Whenever Vietnam or POWs were mentioned inside the White House, it was referred to as "Bud's issue." McFarlane has since admitted to lying to Congress in conjunction with the Iran/contra scandal. He also admitted in the 1985 Evans-Novak Forum that there were POWs alive in Southeast Asia and that the U.S. government had not "even begun to start to do enough to solve the problem." Yet, at the same time, McFarlane was preparing speeches and letters for President Reagan claiming that no administration had done as much as had the Reagan administration. While privately admitting that there was basically "no on-the-ground intelligence" being used in Southeast Asia, McFarlane had Reagan write to Mrs. Duke that "intelligence priorities and assets are at their highest level." These untruths aren't as shocking as Reagan's blind acceptance of them.

McFarlane, Armitage, and Gregg ran these Vietnam-related issues from 1982 through 1985. Admiral John Poindexter replaced McFarlane as National Security Advisor in December 1985. At that point, Armitage moved his deputy at the Pentagon, James Kelly, over to the NSC staff. Colonel Childress, ever the loyal "gopher," remained, serving directly under Kelly.

After the Irangate revelations and the removal of Poindexter, another Armitage crony, Frank Carlucci, was brought in to restore order in the White House national security apparatus. This appointment was curious in that Carlucci was running Sears World Trade, a Sears subsidiary devoted to international arms dealing.

Under Carlucci, Sears World Trade had lost millions of dollars. A former deputy director of the CIA, Carlucci cleaned house at the NSC with one noticeable exception: the Asian Desk. The only directors not to be removed or transferred were Jim Kelly and Richard Childress. And, despite protestations from Tower and Whitehead, who warned the national security advisor in an April 1987 telephone call that the Vietnam issue was "a ticking time bomb waiting to explode at the NSC," Carlucci continued to defer to Richard Armitage's decisions on all matters pertaining to Vietnam. When Texas billionaire and long-time advocate of the POWs, H. Ross Perot, urged a personnel change regarding the administration team dealing with Vietnam in a White House meeting, Carlucci angrily responded to Perot, "Hey, lay off Rich Armitage. He is absolutely essential to the running of the U.S. government."

With this continued endorsement and virtual carte blanche to operate, the Armitage-Gregg-Kelly-Childress team maintained a stranglehold on all Vietnam issues inside the Reagan administration. They extended their reach downward, as well. For example, all personnel throughout the government who dealt with any Vietnam-related foreign policy issues were selected by this Armitage-led team. No one who dissented with their policy was allowed to participate in any discussions or policy meetings. Those who carried out the policy also followed the standard line.

A good case in point is Lt. Col. Paul Mather, an air force officer who, incredibly, was stationed in the same post for fourteen years, without ever being assigned elsewhere. Since the mid-1970s, Mather ran the Bangkok branch of the Joint Casualty Resolution Center (JCRC), formed after the Vietnam War to account for the MIAs. Mather's job was to coordinate the collection of any field information that came into Thailand from refugees fleeing Vietnam, Laos, or Kampuchea. Mather and his staff were to question these refugees, collate the information, and then forward it to the Pentagon in Washington. Curiously, in late 1981, Mather admitted to me and another Republican congressman that he took all intelligence reports about possible living POWs to the "third floor," where the CIA station is located, before forwarding that information to Washington. Mather also admitted that it was the CIA station chief's decision whether or not to transmit this intelligence information to Washington. Why was a supposed-Pentagon employee sharing information first with the CIA and even allowing the CIA to decide what information is given to his superiors?

Regardless of how well Mather may or may not have performed his duties, clearly it is unusual for any military officer to remain in the same post for fourteen uninterrupted years. Obviously his superiors were either incapable of finding a replacement or else judged Mather to be uniquely indispensable. Or he cleverly ingratiated himself with some in Washington who had the ultimate political power to order Mather's military superiors to keep him in Bangkok. Or Mather was not truly a military officer; like North, he was only using the cover of an air force uniform, but in reality worked for some other U.S. intelligence entity.

Members of Congress requested Mather's transfer. Family members of missing men asked for Mather to be moved. And normal military rotation rules demand that an officer not remain in any one post that long. Yet, despite this, Mather continued in the JCRC office in Bangkok until June 1988. He developed an unusually close relationship with Assistant Secretary of Defense Richard Armitage. He became an integral member of the Casey-Armitage team.

Those who deviated from the Armitage group's Vietnam policy were dealt with swiftly. For example, in 1981, based on highly classified intelligence information from satellite and overflight photography and on-the-ground human intelligence, a rescue mission was planned by an intelligence unit inside the Pentagon. The goal was to recover a known group of American POWs held in Laos, probably under Vietnamese control. Actual training and field preparation were underway and a date for the mission was set. However, despite this commitment and the overwhelming evidence supporting the plan, Armitage canceled the mission, threatening to transfer or fire anyone who talked about it.

Similarly, in 1986, the Defense Intelligence Agency, stung by charges of ineptitude, apathy, and cover-up, appointed a blue-ribbon panel of military and intelligence experts to reexamine the evidence concerning the existence of possible POWs held anywhere in Southeast Asia. The panel's chairman was former DIA director Eugene Tighe. General Tighe's group worked for months, poring over hundreds of case files. By late summer, they were prepared to announce their almost unanimous agreement that there definitely were living POWs held against their will in Southeast Asia. However, once again Richard Armitage entered the scene and pressured the present director of the DIA, Gen. Leonard Peroots, to urge Tighe to water down his conclusion. Thus the publicly announced report claimed that all the commission members agreed that American soldiers were alive in Southeast Asia, thereby offering the possibility that these Americans were not prisoners but had stayed behind "voluntarily."

This was an old Armitage ploy; in March 1982, it appeared that three U.S. Navy pilots were about to be privately rescued in central Laos. Armitage quickly provided a backup strategy in the event these men emerged from fifteen years of captivity. Armitage briefed the national news media and ordered the U.S. ambassador to Thailand, John Gunther Dean, to say that, "yes, there are some Americans still in Laos. But they are all either drug addicts or defectors."

Another instance where the Casey team or Armitage group cleverly influenced administration Vietnam policy occurred in April 1987. President Reagan was being heavily pressured by close supporters and advisors, such as Paul Laxalt, Richard Nixon, and Bill Simon, to appoint a special envoy to handle all negotiations with Hanoi on the POW issue. The Armitage group, knowing they couldn't stop this move, decided to participate in the selection of the envoy. They succeeded by advocating retired general John Vessey and then surrounding him totally with Casey team members. Thus, in August 1987, when Vessey journeyed to Hanoi, all the members of his party were team members: Childress, Deputy Assistant Secretary of State David Lambertson, and two other minor officials. Once in Vietnam, these team members refused to allow Vessey to negotiate with the Vietnamese leaders. Whenever the general broached the subject of linking normalized relations with the recovery of living POWs, the team members interrupted and immediately called for a recess. The Vietnamese leadership was amazed. Vessey, after returning to Washington, told me in his Pentagon office, "I don't want anything more to do with that situation." Thus the team had won again, and they intended to continue to formulate and run U.S. policy toward Vietnam despite the outcome of the November presidential election. David Lambertson announced in July 1988 that regardless of which party won the election, he would remain in his present position for two years, running the interagency group that formulates and implements policy regarding Vietnam.

The dominance within the foreign policy-making machinery of one small group, headed by Armitage, Gregg, and Kelly, with Childress carrying out their orders, and supported by a handful of almost permanent employees such as Paul Mather and Lambertson, combined with repeated instances of their either denying, changing, or covering up information about POWs still held against their will in Southeast Asia, leads to one question: Why? Why did this group refuse to allow dissent—and why did they apparently keep the lid on the truth regarding the existence of living American prisoners?

The answer is that this group of former CIA and intelligence officers shared a common experience: the Vietnam War. This group saw the war lost, not on the battlefield, but in Congress and on the streets of the United States. Civilians and politicians pulled the rug out from underneath the soldiers. Despite this, the Vietnam War could still be won through the economic and diplomatic isolation of Vietnam. In other words, by cutting the Hanoi regime off from the outside world, Vietnam's domestic economy would crumble from within. What the United States could not do militarily, it could cause through a complete embargo. The POW issue, specifically the case of American prisoners still alive, is the one issue that has given Hanoi a carrot with which to attract U.S. interest and U.S. economic assistance. This Armitage-led group always feared that if Hanoi and Washington were ever to reach an accord for the return of these prisoners in return for diplomatic normalization, a lifting of the trade embargo, and economic assistance, then Hanoi's regime would be resuscitated. Again, America's "weak-kneed civilian politicians" would have lost the Vietnam War.

## IV

The combination of President Reagan's uninvolved management style and the aggressive, purposeful agenda of the Casey team created the environment in which a "secret foreign policy" was easy to conduct. With a president and a secretary of state more devoted to Central America and to improving relations with the Soviet Union than to Southeast Asia, it was easy for the team to take over the foreign policy machinery for their own purposes.

The checks and balances system built into our government failed. Congress, also averse to addressing Vietnam even years after the end of the war, closed its eyes to administration policies. The national news media failed to draw the obvious analogy with the Iran/contra scandal. For example, after the Tower report's strong recommendation that the national security advisor should not be an active-duty military officer, the team brazenly succeeded in placing one of their own, Gen. Colin Powell, in that position. (Powell had worked closely with Armitage in the Pentagon on the transfer of military arms to the CIA for shipment to Iran and was one of only a handful even aware of the secret plan.) The media virtually ignored the implications of Powell's appointment, thereby increasing the team's arrogance.

The national media, in a rare spate of self-criticism after the Iran/contra revelations, which originally emanated from a Beirut weekly, has admitted to "missing the Iran/contra story." The *Washington Post*'s Bob Woodward sheepishly owned up by admitting to a fellow reporter, "It was under my nose the whole time. . . . All the pieces were there. I just never put it all together." Similarly, other reporters have described pressure from editors to meet short-term deadlines. Apparently, this precluded them from investing time and energy in a longer-term story which required spade work.

Whatever the reason, just as the media missed the Iran/contra affair, they have completely overlooked the obvious inconsistencies and misrepresentations of the team. In an administration that formulated policy according to instant public opinion, this lack of media scrutiny compounded the problem and allowed the team to operate under Reagan's nose, with the president never hearing the truth.

According to Bob Woodward's book *Veil*, Bill Casey, at the outset of the first Reagan term, gleefully said, "I want to win one" back from the Communists. Not only did he and his team of devoted, true-believing hard-liners fail to win anything, they also broke the law, lied to the American people, tolerated and even contributed to the growing Soviet influence in Southeast Asia, and abandoned our brave POWs in Asia.

Not only did the Casey team not "win one," they missed a golden opportunity in Southeast Asia to move Hanoi away from the Soviet orbit and to weaken Moscow's Pacific strategy.

# 6

# THE DOMESTIC IMPLICATIONS OF RECOGNIZING VIETNAM

## I

Only the president of the United States has the constitutional power to normalize relations with another nation. It is unlikely that any president, either Republican or Democrat, would take that step toward Hanoi if he or she were to incur damaging political repercussions. Thus, the questions are: What are the domestic political implications of normalizing relations with a nation who handed the United States its first war defeat? Will recognition become a big political issue? Will it earn the president the title of "Red-lover," or will it provoke mostly yawns from the American people?

In the summer of 1987, President Reagan's pollster, Dr. Richard Wirthlin, conducted a national survey of public opinion on this and other Vietnam-related issues. The results present a clear road map for any president, regardless of party. Of all the bilateral issues that prevent normalization of relations, the recovery of living American POWs is the one that most interests the clear majority of Americans. Seventy-four percent view the POWs as the most important issue; only 13 percent selected Vietnamese withdrawal from Kampuchea, and only 4 percent view the recovery of remains as important.

Just twelve years after the fall of Saigon and the United States' humiliating final withdrawal by helicopter from the top of the U.S. embassy, a surprisingly large number of Americans, 36 percent, favor normalizing relations with Hanoi before the POW/MIA issue is settled. In other words, over one-third of the American people favor taking this step, despite a decade of negative publicity about the Hanoi regime and, conversely, nothing positive being said in favor of normalization.

Any president willing to take this first step would undoubtedly pave the way by preparing the people for this move. This "suasion," or use of the "bully pulpit," would increase support for this sudden change in policy, just as a presidential plea almost always influences public support for a presidential decision.

When President Richard Nixon took the utterly surprising first step of announcing renewed contact with Communist China and a subsequent trip to Peking, the public, the media, and Congress were flabbergasted. Everyone was not only shocked at the secretiveness leading up to this announcement, but also shocked that Richard Nixon, the "life-long anti-Communist," who had become a national figure by exposing Alger Hiss as a Communist in the State Department, would be the president to open a new era of relations with the largest Communist nation on earth. Of course, Nixon had more political credibility, as a hard-liner, to make this move. Similarly, only Menachem Begin, as the hard-line Israeli prime minister, could reach a peace agreement with Egypt. Both Nixon and Begin had their right flank covered by decades of trench warfare locked arm-in-arm with the right wing of their party. Thus, they could safely move to the center for a controversial step on foreign policy.

Normalizing relations with Vietnam does not immediately carry the geopolitical significance of either the China move or the Camp David Accords, but it can, in the long run, greatly influence the future course of events in Asia. American reactions, though, will be less analytical and more emotional, based on the terrible scars of the Vietnam War. A president needs to demonstrate to the people in what way it is in the United States' interest to normalize relations with Hanoi.

The Wirthlin survey indicates that, even without making these arguments, much of the nation is already a receptive audience. For example, 41 percent of Republicans favor normalization. Thus it is unlikely that the more conservative of the two parties is likely to make a huge national issue out of this move. Similarly, 58 percent of people with postgraduate degrees and 51 percent of college graduates already favor normalization. Perhaps this comes from knowing exactly what "normalization" is. These better-educated people know that normalization is not analogous to granting a stamp of approval on Hanoi or on Hanoi's policies. It merely means that we are willing to recognize the Vietnamese regime as the government of the Vietnamese people, and thus we will talk to them in a civil manner.

With a majority of better-educated people already supporting normalization, this step probably would earn the backing of many opinion leaders, newspaper columnists, editorial writers, and educational authorities. Thus, an entire "sales force" is in place to support this plan.

Many on-the-air media personalities today were battlefield correspondents during the war. They all have their own opinions on the war and U.S. conduct since. Many would now agree that it is time to change our policy. These television personalities are the single most powerful group of opinion leaders in the nation. From the morning shows on all three networks to the national evening news, the Sunday programs, and talk shows, this decision is bound to be debated. But, if the news personalities and hosts are inclined toward this new policy, then an open-minded public is more than likely to accept it.

What about Congress? Surprisingly, a large number of the younger conservative Republicans in the House of Representatives—previously derided as "Reagon robots"—are already arguing for normalization, on the theory that this will help break the logjam on the POW/MIA issue. Similarly, but for different reasons, many senior liberal senators, ranging from Senate Foreign Relations Chairman Claiborne Pell to Republican Mark Hatfield, also argue in favor of the recognition of Hanoi. Between these congressional extremes are hundreds of members from both parties who know very little about this issue but are always sensitive to anything that could be emotionally and politically explosive.

For example, many representatives are aware of the growing size and influence of the Indochinese refugee population now living in the United States. By the end of 1987, over 800,000 Vietnamese, Cambodians, and Laotians lived in the United States. Many of these people have just become citizens and therefore are eligible to vote for the first time. Because they escaped tyrannical Communist regimes, it is thought that this group will vote as a bloc of anti-

Communist hard-liners. There is no evidence yet to back up this theory, but ironically, this potential has forced some previously liberal congressmen to sound like born-again conservatives when it comes to Hanoi. For example, the liberal Democrat, Representative Chester Atkins of Massachusetts, claims over 20,000 Indochinese voters in his district. He has begun to sound like a born-again hawk on Vietnam-related issues. He opposes diplomatic normalization until Hanoi's forces withdraw from Kampuchea and until Vietnam does more on the POW/MIA issue—the same position as the conservative Reagan administration.

In the 1988 presidential campaign, attempts were being made on both sides to form an Indochinese bloc vote. The Vietnam Veterans Coalition, a group of U.S. veterans groups, made a nationwide attempt to join forces with anti-Communist Indochinese group leaders to produce a unified voice to speak on all issues related to the war—from Agent Orange to funding the resistance movements to settling the POW/MIA issue. This group has a conservative Republican tilt. On the other side, Massachusetts governor Michael Dukakis was supported by a southern California Indochinese group that held a fund-raising event that raised over forty thousand dollars for his presidential campaign.

As U.S. congressmen pay political attention to Indochinese voters, the issues that will emerge are familiar ones. For instance, should the United States finance the resistance movements in Kampuchea, Laos, and Vietnam? This same debate raged over the Nicaraguan contras and, to a much lesser degree, over the Angolan and Afghan freedom fighters. The difference in this instance is that the move toward supporting the Kampuchean resistance comes not from the Right, but from the liberals. The charge has been led by left-wing congressman Stephen Solarz, who sponsored a House measure to provide $5 million to the non-Communist segment of the Khmer Rouge fighting against the Vietnamese in Kampuchea. Representing the supposedly conservative Reagan administration, Secretary of State George Shultz opposed this aid.

Another pivotal domestic U.S. political issue for these new voters centers on the continuing attempt by Japanese businessmen to invest in, and trade with, Vietnam. These Japanese recognize that Vietnam can become a mini-China with a sizable work force that features hard work and discipline as staples of their society. There is good potential for quality cheap labor and for a growing market. The Japanese have repeatedly attempted to strike lucrative deals with the regime in Hanoi. Japanese newspapers have reported proposed Japanese investments in Vietnam totaling $4 billion.

When these attempted arrangements become public, U.S. politicians jump, as when Wisconsin senator Robert Kasten spoke out against the massive building and investment program Honda of Japan planned in Vietnam. Honda soon relented and abandoned the deal. As Japanese-bashing becomes more prevalent in the United States, it will become increasingly popular to attack any Japanese investment in Vietnam. This will appeal not only to the growing Indochinese vote but also to other Americans who seek to blame the Japanese for the U.S. trade deficit and the loss of jobs.

## II

The 1980s have seen a reevaluation of the Vietnam War, the leaders who conducted that effort, and the way the media covered it. Some opinions have changed; others have hardened. Rambo has become a hero, Jane Fonda more of a villain. Even General William Westmoreland has been rehabilitated. The Vietnam Veterans Memorial Wall has been built. Parades finally welcoming home our troops have helped to soften the bitterness of their original return. Movies like *Platoon, Hamburger Hill,* and *Full Metal Jacket* show conflicting accounts of the war itself.

The United States has finally been able to look back on one of the worst periods in our nation's history. While the pain will never leave, it has receded enough to allow rational analysis. However, there is no sense in looking back unless we apply those lessons to the future. The question of normalizing relations with Vietnam and then moving toward a new, warmer relationship with the Hanoi regime is the next logical step in the healing process. If the United States can rebuild both Japan and West Germany, not out of sentimentality or guilt, but because of the strategic significance of both nations, then the United States must also recognize the value of Vietnam in Southeast Asia. To continue to consign Vietnam to the Soviet orbit is bad policy for the United States and for U.S. interests.

Whichever president of the United States decides to take the first step and normalize relations with Vietnam can make a strong argument to the American people that this decision is in the best long-term interests of the United States. Yes, it will facilitate the settlement of bilateral matters such as the POW/MIA and Amerasian children issues, but longer-term American interests lie in winning the peaceful battle against Moscow, fought not on the battlefield but through trade, diplomacy, and international economics. Presented in that light, the U.S. domestic Right can be satisfied with the decision to normalize relations with Hanoi.

If the American people are reevaluating the Vietnam era, some elements of the federal bureaucracy are still fighting the Vietnam War. It is with these groups, blocs, and internal constituencies that a president will have the most difficulty with the normalization of relations with Vietnam. Specifically, elements within the Pentagon and the intelligence community will try to play bureaucratic games to stop diplomatic recognition. These groups, comprised of hardliners and unreconstructed war hawks, still bitter over civilian politicians pulling the rug out from underneath the American soldiers in Vietnam, will leak, stall, and obfuscate in an attempt to block any presidential decision to normalize relations with Hanoi.

In 1978, when President Carter contemplated the normalization of relations with Hanoi, he met his strongest opposition inside his own administration, specifically inside the Pentagon and the CIA. A similar situation existed in 1971 when President Nixon and his national security advisor, Henry Kissinger, conducted their own private outreach to Peking, without the State Department or the Defense Department knowing anything about the operation. President Nixon and Kissinger only met and discussed the China breakthrough in the family dining room, out of reach of even other close White House advisors. Nixon knew Washington. He was aware that a few well-timed leaks could scuttle the whole China initiative before it even began. By keeping the plan secret, Nixon was able to go directly to the American people on television and rally their support before his potential opponents inside Washington had even heard of the operation.

Now, fifteen years after that first presidential visit to Peking, those hard-line groups in the Defense Department who were aghast that Richard Nixon, of all people, would become friendly with

Mao Tse Tung are the strongest supporters of better relations with China. Whoever would have thought that Weinberger, the most vocal anti-Communist defense secretary in recent memory, would lead the charge for arms sales to China? Because Weinberger was "on board" this policy, the Right protested very little.

Normalization of relations with Vietnam bears other similarities to the China recognition. For example, the U.S. business community heavily supported the Nixon move in the early 1970s. The prospect of competing in a billion-person market excites any businessman. Vietnam, of course, is much smaller, but the Vietnamese are desperate for many U.S. exports, ranging from basic foodstuffs to agricultural products such as tractors, fertilizers, and chemicals.

Vietnam also needs to build new infrastructures such as sewers, roads, bridges, and a modern telephone system. High technology, as well, is a goal of the Linh regime. To address these shortcomings, the Vietnamese government in late 1987 finally adopted a new investment code that offers foreign investors some of the best incentives in Asia. Foreign businessmen can own 99 percent of a business placed inside Vietnam and can repatriate all profits. This capitalistic plan is yet another example of Linh's mandate to restructure and improve the domestic economy as quickly as possible.

U.S. business investment in Vietnam should be encouraged, not blocked. The trade embargo should be lifted as part of a schedule of actions to follow the initial normalization of relations. Once U.S. businesses study the new situation, they will see in Vietnam not just a growing market, but the availability of cheap labor that is well disciplined, eager, and economically motivated. Many U.S. veterans of the Vietnam War have commented that if "you could channel the Vietnamese battlefield spirit into workplace spirit, you'll have the best workers anywhere."

Richard Nixon's China initiative was planned to be a key ingredient in his 1972 reelection campaign. The Peking visit provided excellent television coverage of the president acting as statesman; the American media and people were enthralled. The announcement of normalization of relations with Hanoi will not provide the same domestic political benefit to a president. As U.S. ambassador Angier Biddle Duke, an intimate of several presidents, said to me, "Recognition of the Hanoi government is an idea whose time has come. But any candidate for president will wait until after the election. The best time to make this move is early in the first year of a new administration."

Politically, the optimum time for such a decision and announcement is probably during the "honeymoon" period of a new presidency, when Congress and the media tend to accept new policies and programs without so much criticism as later, when the next election looms just over the horizon.

## III

U.S. domestic politics are rife with inconsistencies. For example, while the U.S. surgeon general cautions against smoking, the federal government is doling out hundreds of millions of dollars in tobacco subsidies. Similarly, U.S. foreign policy is filled with inexplicable double standards. Those who have succeeded in isolating Vietnam and labeling Hanoi as an international pariah because of the invasion of Kampuchea are the very same people who dismiss the Soviet invasion of Afghanistan as not important enough to get in the way of an improvement in Soviet-American relations.

For example, the Reagan administration linked any improvement in relations with Vietnam to a total and complete withdrawal of Vietnamese forces from Kampuchea. Yet no such linkage was applied in Detente II between Gorbachev and Reagan. In fact, Reagan dismissed the Afghan situation and excused Gorbachev because "he wasn't in office when the invasion occurred."

Applying that standard, the Kampuchean situation could be overlooked because Vietnamese general secretary Linh was not in office when the invasion was launched. In fact, Linh was purged from the Hanoi government in 1982 for advocating "too radical" domestic reforms.

While Soviet soldiers continued to slaughter Afghan citizens, the Reagan administration announced plans to explore with the Soviets ways to transfer high technology to Moscow. The last Reagan secretary of commerce, William Verity, was a long-time advocate of increased trade with the Soviets—without any linkage to Soviet behavior. Similarly, the Reagan administration also began talks with Moscow on ways to secure Soviet admission to the World Bank, the IMF, and the General Agreement on Tariffs and Trade

(GATT). In each of these instances, the linkage was to Soviet domestic economic reforms, not foreign policy changes. In other words, the Reagan administration tolerated expansionist Soviet conduct around the world, but insisted on domestic alterations; regarding Vietnam, they condemned Hanoi's foreign policy and offered no inducements for Vietnam to change.

Inconsistency is the benchmark of U.S. foreign policy in other regions, as well. While refusing normalized relations with Hanoi, Washington maintains full diplomatic normalization with Nicaragua. The United States continues to maintain an embassy in Managua but, at the same time, funds the anti-Sandinista contra rebels in an attempt to overthrow that Communist government. The Reagan administration daily issued strong condemnations of Nicaragua's behavior, yet even in the early days of the first Reagan term, U.S. foreign aid to Managua exceeded $100 million.

Cuba, long condemned by each U.S. administration for its constant attempt to export revolution in the Western Hemisphere and even in Africa, has more of a formal relationship with Washington than does Hanoi. Both Havana and Washington maintain an interest section in each other's capitols. This semiofficial form of diplomatic contact allows informal, but proper, communication. Interest sections usually are housed in a neutral third country's embassy. In early 1987, Oregon senator Mark Hatfield journeyed to Hanoi and reached agreement with the Swedish ambassador to Vietnam to allow a U.S. interest section to be housed in the Swedish embassy in Hanoi. Upon returning to Washington and presenting this proposal to the Reagan administration, Hatfield was immediately rejected. The White House did not want even that level of official contact with Vietnam.

After the Communist government in Poland crushed the Solidarity Labor movement in 1981, the Reagan administration cut off economic assistance to that regime, but it did not sever diplomatic relations. Similarly, after repeated instances of international terrorism were traced to the Syrian government, the United States took the relatively mild step of temporarily recalling the U.S. ambassador. Again, diplomatic relations were not severed. In the wake of a cease-fire in the Iran-Iraq war, Reagan administration officials indicated a desire to resume full normalized relations with Tehran.

Gross inconsistencies abound in the United States' indirect use of foreign aid, as well. Through the World Bank and the International Monetary Fund, the United States offers billions of dollars in economic assistance to friend and foe alike. For example, the Communist government of Yugoslavia has received $4.7 billion in loans from the World Bank; the Communist government in Romania, $2.2 billion; the Communist government in Hungary, $1.3 billion. The Communist government in Mozambique has received over $160 million. South Yemen, one of Moscow's latest acquisitions in the key location overlooking the Suez Canal, has received $210 million from the World Bank.

What is the logic behind making huge sums available to these tyrannical, Communist, Moscow-backed dictatorships but refusing any aid to Vietnam? Why not use economic incentives, both directly from Washington and indirectly through these U.S.-supported international financial institutions, to encourage Hanoi to change its behavior and policies? Why not attempt to buy Hanoi away from Moscow, instead of forcing her into Moscow's embrace? Why shouldn't Washington step in to help alleviate Vietnam's economic and debt plight, thereby reducing Hanoi's dependence on Moscow?

During the debate of the Reagan administration's policy toward the government of South Africa, bitterness developed over the "constructive engagement" policy. Critics claimed that this was, in effect, tacit approval of Pretoria's discrimination policies. Defenders of the administration argued that it was better to maintain relations with Pretoria so as to be "in the tent" and able to have some influence over South African policy.

A similar argument now applies to U.S. relations with Vietnam: for the last thirteen years, by refusing to make any positive move toward Hanoi, the United States has actually been practicing "destructive disengagement." By refusing, in any form whatsoever, to get in the tent with Vietnam, we have forced Hanoi into Moscow's tent. The result has been (1) a greatly increased Soviet military presence in the region, (2) a worried and nervous ASEAN, (3) decreased U.S. diplomatic clout in the area, and (4) a complete failure to resolve any of the outstanding bilateral issues between Washington and Hanoi. In other words, the U.S. policy toward Vietnam has brought about the very results Washington wanted to avoid.

## IV

One of the major domestic issues in the United States in the 1990s will be the continuing debate over trade policy. As more and more Americans become frightened over the potential loss of manufacturing jobs to cheaper overseas labor, specifically in Asia, there will be an increased reluctance to assist any Asian nation. Thus, the president who will normalize relations with Hanoi will find that is the easiest part of the package to sell to the American people. After all, sending an ambassador to Hanoi doesn't cost the average U.S. taxpayer much. However, anything more than that, such as aid, loans, or subsidies, will encounter much more political difficulty. That is why the actual normalization should be unilateral, without any attached quid pro quo. The next steps, though, must be tied to specific Vietnamese actions such as definitive progress on bilateral issues and on disengagement from Kampuchea. Only with tit for tat can the president justify further steps and assistance to a nervous American people and Congress.

The one other constituency that will oppose normalization of relations with Hanoi is perhaps the most difficult one for a president to overrule: the professional foreign policy expert. Washington is filled with these self-proclaimed intellectuals, all of whom have either previously served in government or else are angling to serve now. They are located in think tanks or university faculties. They make their living by commenting on any and all White House foreign policy decisions. Many are almost regular guests on "Nightline" and "This Week with David Brinkley."

Presidents have a hard time with this group because most new presidents, with the sole exception of Richard Nixon, arrive in office with little or no foreign policy background. They soon learn that Congress dominates domestic policy, so the president turns to foreign affairs—and to a stable of these so-called experts for advice. A large majority of these people oppose relations with Vietnam, not for any good reason but simply because they are the very people who have constructed our present policy toward Hanoi. To support change would be to admit the mistakes of this policy.

Thus, the president who wants to recognize Vietnam and move toward a new relationship must not be deterred by the carping and criticism that is inevitable from this group of intelligentsia. In reality, they have no power—and the American people couldn't care less what they say on television.

### V

The United States in the last quarter of the twentieth century has become a nation and a populace dominated by television. This medium not only influences what people think, but also how they think. For instance, the recent success of *People* magazine and *USA Today* are due, in part, to the short-focus period of television news broadcasts. In other words, most people in the United States want the headline and the facts—quickly. Their concentration will stray after a few minutes.

Similarly, television news has adopted the habit of only pursuing a story for more than a day or two if "it has legs." Iran/contra had "legs" because each day brought a new revelation. However, once most of the story was out on the table, it couldn't be sustained any longer. It disappeared. Within a matter of a few days, it was a distant memory.

In judging the impact of the political decision to normalize relations with Vietnam, an administration should know that it is, in the vernacular, at best a two- or three-day story. The announcement itself will earn attention. The reaction, both in the United States and around the world, will dominate the second day. The third day might contain reactions from select groups, such as U.S. war veterans, family members of POWs, or former South Vietnamese officials now living in the United States. After the third day, the story will no longer appear on the front page or at the top of the network television news. It will already have become old news.

Recognizing Vietnam will not bring riots on the streets; instead, it will cause many Americans to debate a serious topic, without the raw emotions of years gone by. At the centerpiece of this national discussion should be one overriding criterion: what is in the best interests of the United States?

# 7

# CONCLUSION: THINGS THAT MUST BE DONE IMMEDIATELY

## I

The United States needs to arouse itself from its post-Vietnam slumber and realize that the Pacific is the world's fastest growing region. Washington needs to adjust its thinking, remembering that the United States remains the leading economic power in the world. For too long American myopia has consigned Southeast Asia to a competiton between the Soviets and the Chinese.

The United States should immediately change policy and focus its diplomatic energy on reentering the competition in Southeast Asia. To do so, Washington should adopt the following measures:

**A.** Unilaterally normalize relations with Hanoi, despite short-term protestations from some of our ASEAN friends and allies. In recognizing Vietnam, Washington should not automatically grant full trading privileges to Hanoi, but instead should announce a schedule of increased trade and economic assistance to Hanoi, pro-vided Hanoi announces a schedule of progress on resolving the bilateral issues mentioned above. Included in this announced sched-ule by Washington should be incentives, such as accelerated assis-tance, most favored nation trading status, and help with the World Bank and the International Montary Fund. Also, incentives should be included to encourage Hanoi to use its unique relationship with Laos and Kampuchea to settle once and for all the POW/MIA situation in those two countries as well.

Future trade schedules and economic concessions should be tied to the three other main bilateral issues, the Amerasian children, the release of political prisoners, and the acceleration of the Orderly Departure Program. Hanoi should be encouraged to repatriate the children of U.S. soldiers and rewarded for allowing citizens to leave. Emigration is, and has been, the central impediment to increased trade with the Soviets; why not the same for Vietnam?

Washington should recognize that the best way to encourage Hanoi to change is not by threatening it, but by offering positive inducements and rewards for actions with which the United States agrees. Furthermore, Hanoi must now be treated not with bitterness, but in the spirit of a new diplomatic relationship that can benefit both sides. The United States should contrast its behavior to that of its "clumsy rival," Moscow.

**B.** The United States should encourage private U.S. investment in Vietnam. This is especially true in the short term as Congress struggles with a massive federal deficit and a 20 percent cut in the foreign aid budget. Businesses throughout Asia already recognize that Vietnam offers not just a large work force, but a potentially lucrative market, as well. Turning the Vietnamese spirit away from war making and toward product making can only benefit everyone. The success in China in the last decade of adopting semifree market innovations is certain to be duplicated by Hanoi. General Secretary Linh is a pragmatic leader who recognizes that Deng and Gorbachev have already taken huge steps to reform their systems. Linh is also inclined to adopt reforms, especially with U.S. assistance, and, as he does so, he will gradually move away from the Soviet orbit. Hanoi will move because only the United States can satisfy Vietnam's economic and technological needs, ranging from fertilizer to personal computers. Hanoi's change of direction, however, can only occur with constant, positive U.S. prodding, not the bullying, threatening behavior of the Soviets.

The United States, as a superpower, should not surrender in any contest, not even on the terms of the debate. In other words, Washington should compete for a new preeminence in Southeast Asia on its own terms, not those of the Soviets. Thus, U.S. economic might can triumph over Soviet military power, if Washington works hand in hand with the U.S. and Asian business community to encourage a new economic offensive in the region, beginning with Vietnam. Japan recently unveiled plans for just such an offensive, including a possible $4 billion investment program for Vietnam. (The United States has pressured Tokyo not to trade with Hanoi.)

**C.** Washington should substantially increase military and economic assistance to its front-line ally, Thailand. Such an increase will be correctly interpreted by Thailand as a strong signal that the United States has no intention of allowing a newly resurgent Vietnam to take advantage of this new United States–Vietnamese relationship to cause trouble for Thailand. Hanoi, as well, during the initial stages of this new relationship, needs to be alerted that Washington has hedged its bet by insuring the security of its ally in Bangkok.

**D.** After normalizing relations with Hanoi, Washington and ASEAN will continue to press for a Vietnamese withdrawal from Kampuchea. While it is doubtful that Hanoi will immediately relinquish control of Kampuchea, the United States should encourage this withdrawal by increasing its military assistance to the Son Sann–led National Liberation Front forces within the anti-Hanoi resistance movement. This support, too, will be a signal to Hanoi that, while Washington wants a new, positive relationship with Vietnam, Washington will not accept the invasion of a sovereign state. Reductions in this military assistance should be made only if directly tied to Vietnamese withdrawal of troops from Kampuchea.

Washington should also use its diplomatic clout with Beijing to prevent the return to power in Kampuchea of Pol Pot or the Khmer Rouge. Hanoi has privately requested that the United States enter this issue forcefully, so as to allow an orderly departure of Vietnamese troops from Kampuchea.

**E.** The United States should recognize the inevitable and help bring it about. Beijing and Hanoi, once close, will have to reach some sort of new understanding, probably short of friendship but certainly warmer than present relations. Washington, after normalizing relations with Hanoi and launching a new economic relationship with Vietnam, should exert its diplomatic muscle and act as a good faith intermediary between China and Vietnam. All three nations ultimately have the same goal: a lessening Soviet presence in Southeast Asia. Hanoi will be ready to play its own China card with Moscow once the United States has a stake in a new relationship with Vietnam.

Moscow, struggling today with its own economic restructuring, will not be able to compete in Southeast Asia with a renewed U.S. economic presence. The Soviets, frustrated by their own economic impotence and their suddenly less attractive and less needed military power, will find themselves dealt out of the region. Vietnam, relieved of its Kampuchean burden and profiting by lessened hostility from China, will naturally grow less reliant on Moscow.

The ASEAN nations will applaud this new U.S. diplomatic and economic offensive. Undoubtedly, Indonesia and Malaysia will be nervous about a possible China-Vietnam rapprochement, but that apprehension will be offset by the increased U.S. role in the region. The opening of the Vietnamese market and the harnessing of the Vietnamese discipline and spirit will offer ASEAN businesses numerous new opportunities and benefits.

Southeast Asia will adopt a new, natural multialignment system, with various nations joining together for certain goals. A shifting equilibrium will result, born of natural competition. The centerpiece of this system must be a free-enterprise system.

This concept of a Pacific community can only succeed with the participation of all the region's nations, including Vietnam. Ultimately, only the United States can welcome Vietnam back into not only the Pacific community, but the world community. It must be Washington's goal, as it is Hanoi's, that Vietnam not be subordinate to either Moscow or Beijing. Only the United States can bring about that result.

Beyond geopolitical strategies and economic interplay, the other argument in favor of the diplomatic normalization of relations between Washington and Hanoi was best expressed to me in Vietnam by the deputy foreign minister, Nguyen Dy Nien. As we drank traditional Vietnamese green tea, Minister Nien said, "Even though the war is over, the bleeding continues on both sides. Only the normalization of relations can stop the bleeding."

# APPENDIXES

## APPENDIX A
## FORMER PRESIDENT NIXON'S MESSAGE TO
## PRIME MINISTER PHAM VAN DONG
## (STATE DEPARTMENT ANNOUNCEMENT)

The department released on May 19, 1977, the text of a message dated February 1, 1973, from former president Nixon to the prime minister of the former Democratic Republic of Vietnam, Pham Van Dong. The existence and substance of this document have already been made public, including public references by the recipient. Its author has indicated no objection to its release. In light of all present circumstances, we have determined that the message is no longer deemed sensitive, and it has been declassified.

**Text of the message from the president of the United States to the prime minister of the Democratic Republic of Vietnam**

**February 1, 1973**

The President wishes to inform the Democratic Republic of Vietnam of the principles which will govern United States participation in the postwar reconstruction of North Vietnam. As indicated in Article 21 of The Agreement on Ending the War and Restoring Peace in Vietnam signed in Paris on January 27, 1973, the United States undertakes this participation in accordance with its traditional policies. These principles are as follows:

1) The Government of the United States of America will contribute to postwar reconstruction in North Vietnam without any political conditions.

2) Preliminary United States studies indicate that the appropriate programs for the United States contribution to postwar reconstruction will fall in the range of $3.25 billion of grant aid over five years. Other forms of aid will be agreed upon between the two parties. This estimate is subject to revision and to detailed discussion between the Government of the United States and the Government of the Democratic Republic of Vietnam.

3) The United States will propose to the Democratic Republic of Vietnam the establishment of a United States–North Vietnamese Joint Economic Commission within 30 days from the date of this message.

4) The function of this Commission will be to develop programs for the United States contribution to reconstruction of North Vietnam. This United States contribution will be based upon such factors as:

(a) The needs of North Vietnam arising from the dislocation of war;

(b) The requirements for postwar reconstruction in the agricultural and industrial sector of North Vietnam's economy.

5) The Joint Economic Commission will have an equal number of representatives from each side. It will agree upon a mechanism to administer the program which will constitute the United States contribution to the reconstruction of North Vietnam. The Commission will attempt to complete this agreement within 60 days after its establishment.

6) The two members of the Commission will function on the principle of respect for each other's sovereignty, non-interference in each other's internal affairs, equality and mutual benefit. The offices of the Commission will be located at a place to be agreed upon by the United States and the Democratic Republic of Vietnam.

7) The United States considers that the implementation of the foregoing principles will promote economic, trade and other relations between the United States of America and the Democratic Republic of Vietnam and will contribute to insuring a stable and lasting peace in Indochina. These principles accord with the spirit of Chapter VIII of The Agreement on Ending the War and Restoring Peace in Vietnam which was signed in Paris on January 27, 1973.

### Understanding Regarding Economic Reconstruction Program

It is understood that the recommendations of the Joint Economic Commission mentioned in the President's note to the Prime Minister will be implemented by each member in accordance with its own constitutional provisions.

## Note Regarding Other Forms of Aid

In regard to other forms of aid, United States studies indicate that the appropriate programs could fall in the range of 1 to 1.5 billion dollars depending on food and other commodity needs of the Democratic Republic of Vietnam.

Department of State Bulletin
June 27, 1977

**APPENDIX B
HEARINGS BEFORE THE HOUSE SELECT
COMMITTEE ON MISSING PERSONS IN
SOUTHEAST ASIA**

Ninety-Fourth Congress
Second Session
Part 5
June 17, 25, July 21, and September 21, 1976
Pages 47–49

*Mr. Gilman:* With regard to that high price, when we were in Hanoi there were references made to some agreements made between our Government and Vietnam with regard to postwar reparations. Can you set forth for us just where we stand with regard to those negotiations? Were there any agreements we are not aware of, secret memorandum that this committee is not aware of?

*Mr. Habib:* There is no agreement or secret memorandum which this committee is not aware of in this respect. There were, as the committee is aware, some letters and exchanges. With respect to those letters, I think the committee has been informed of the content of those letters as they bear on the question which the committee has raised. That is my understanding.

*Mr. McCloskey:* Will the gentleman yield?

*Mr. Gilman:* Yes. I am pleased to yield to the gentleman from California.

*Mr. McCloskey:* With all due respect, Mr. Secretary, this committee asked the Secretary of State and you the same question before we went to Hanoi last December. You did not advise us of that secret letter and we discovered its existence only when we got to Hanoi. Can you tell this committee now why we went to Hanoi without being advised of the existence of that letter which was known to the Secretary of State, especially after we asked you about it?

*Mr. Habib:* I don't recall that we were—were we asked specifically about the letter before you went?

*Mr. McCloskey:* We didn't have any idea the letter existed. We asked you in November if there were any secret agreements that we should know about before we went to Hanoi and we were not advised by you or the Secretary of State of the letter's existence or of the $3.25 billion figure which we later ascertained.

*Mr. Habib:* That is not an agreement. It never developed into an agreement.

Very frankly, Mr. Congressman, I didn't know of the existence of the letter at that time either.

*Mr. McCloskey:* But the Department knew of the existence of the letter. That is one of the frustrations with which this committee has had to contend. We ask for facts and we are answered by people who say, "We don't know."

*Mr. Habib:* I am not saying I don't know in response to your question. Let me make the answer very specific. There is no agreement, there was no agreement, there never was an agreement as far as I know, and I think I would know at this stage. We have researched it and there is no agreement with respect to the question of aid involved in that letter.

That letter was simply a letter primarily designed to set up a Joint Economic Commission pursuant to article 21 of the Paris agreement. The truth of the matter is there was no agreement.

*Mr. Gilman:* If the gentleman will yield . . . Would it be possible to present that letter and make it part of our committee's records since there has been such an issue raised with regard to the correspondence? We learned about it for the first time when we were in Hanoi and the Vietnamese officials referred to that letter.

*Mr. Habib:* I think that is a question which has been raised previously. I will take it back with me, but as you know it involves something which is not within my personal prerogative to respond to, that is a question of Presidential correspondence. But I will provide an answer to that question to the committee.[1]

*Mr. Gilman:* Mr. Chairman, I ask that at this portion of the record the letter be inserted provided State furnishes that letter to the committee.

*The Chairman:* We would like to get the letter.

*Mr. Habib:* I have responded that I will take the question and I have given you the answer that we have had previously that there are other issues involved and a question of Presidential correspondence which I am not in a position to respond to right now but I will respond to the committee. Exactly how I will respond will depend on the general issue involved and the position the administration takes.

*Mr. Gilman:* Without objection, may that letter be inserted?

*The Chairman:* Without objection, if we get the letter.

*Mr. Ottinger:* We have previously requested the letter which I understand

[1]At the time of publication, the Select Committee had not received the Nixon letter.

is now under the control of the National Security Council. The Secretary of State said at a press conference that the offer of some $3.35 billion of aid was of course conditioned upon certain performance by the North Vietnamese actions with respect to the war that was continuing and congressional approval. If that is the case it seems to me it would be of advantage to the administration to have that known. The inference we have to draw is that the case is as the North Vietnamese stated to us, the letter represented an unconditional pledge. I think it would be very much to the advantage of the Government to have it released unless that letter is embarrassing. If that letter is embarrassing it seems to me that is something we ought to know.

*The Chairman:* Mr. Secretary, could we take about a 10-minute break? It might be longer. We have a vote. We will continue this discussion. The committee will be in recess for 10 minutes.

[Short recess.]

*The Chairman:* The committee will come to order. Without objection, Mr. Guyer, I yield to you for some questions.

*Mr. Guyer:* Thank you, Mr. Chairman. I would like to just address a couple of questions, if I might, on the heels of what was said just a moment ago. It seems the letter, the missing document we have asked the Secretary for many, many times, and which he has said repeatedly there was no such agreement made, relating to a pledge in dollars. That matter I think, has been handled now since it has been made a part of the record.

But let me say this in behalf of the families and their concerns. On numerous occasions the Secretary has said he does not trust nor accept the word of the North Vietnamese. Then shouldn't we be consistent in not accepting their word when they say there are no Americans there?

[Applause.]

## APPENDIX C
## WIRTHLIN SURVEY

Now, let's change the subject and talk about an issue that has been in the news lately . . .

1. There has been some discussion recently regarding this country's relationship with Vietnam.

   I'd like to read you some issues of concern regarding the United States and Vietnam, and please tell me which *one* of them you believe is most important for the two countries to address: (ROTATE—READ SLOWLY—CIRCLE ONE ONLY)

| | |
|---|---|
| Getting Vietnam to withdraw from Cambodia | 13% |
| Recovering possible living U.S. prisoners of war | 73% |
| Digging up crash sites and recovering remains of U.S. servicemen, or | 6% |
| Helping more Vietnamese refugees come to the United States | 4% |

2. Now, I'd like you to tell me whether you agree or disagree with the following statement concerning this issue:

   The Reagan Administration has done all it could to determine if prisoners of war are still being held in Vietnam and Laos.
   (WAIT FOR RESPONSE THEN ASK:) Would that be strongly (agree/disagree) or just somewhat (agree/disagree)?

| | |
|---|---|
| SRONGLY AGREE | 10% |
| SOMEWHAT AGREE | 13% |
| SOMEWHAT DISAGREE | 29% |
| STRONGLY DISAGREE | 41% |

3. Now, do you believe there are living U.S. prisoners of war held against their will in Vietnam and Laos?

| | |
|---|---|
| YES (ASK QS.4–5) | 82% |
| NO (GO TO Q.6) | 8% |
| DON'T KNOW/UNSURE (ASK QS.4–5) | 11% |

IF "YES" OR "DON'T KNOW/UNSURE" ON Q.3, ASK QS. 4 & 5:

4. Now, I'd like you to tell me whether you agree or disagree with the following statement concerning this issue:

The Reagan Administration is doing all it can to recover these possible prisoners of war.

(WAIT FOR RESPONSE, THEN ASK:) Would that be strongly (agree/disagree) or just somewhat (agree/disagree)?

| | |
|---|---|
| STRONGLY AGREE | 11% |
| SOMEWHAT AGREE | 14% |
| SOMEWHAT DISAGREE | 30% |
| STRONGLY DISAGREE | 41% |

5. Some people have charged that our Government is covering up the truth about possible POWs still held alive in Vietnam.
Do you think there is or is not a cover-up?

| | |
|---|---|
| YES/COVER-UP | 59% |
| NO | 27% |
| DON'T KNOW/NO ANSWER | 14% |

6. Now I'm going to read you two different positions concerning this issue. Some people say that in order to settle the POW issue, the U.S. and Vietnam first need to normalize relations and exchange ambassadors, just like the United States already does with the Soviet Union and China.

Others say that the POW Issue must be settled *before* relations between the U.S. and Vietnam are normalized.

What about you? Do you believe the U.S. and Vietnam should normalize relations *prior* to solving the POW question, or should the POW issue be settled *first*?

NORMALIZE RELATIONS FIRST                          36%

POW ISSUE FIRST                                    56%

DON'T KNOW/NO ANSWER                                8%

# GLOSSARY

*ASEAN:* Association of Southeast Asian Nations, comprising Thailand, Indonesia, the Philippines, Brunei, Singapore, and Malaysia.

*Hanoi:* The capital city of Vietnam.

*Kampuchea:* Cambodia.

*Laos:* The small Asian nation on Vietnam's western border. In order to control Laos, Vietnam has stationed between 40,000 and 100,000 soldiers in this country of 91,500 square miles.

*National Security Council (NSC):* The executive branch group consisting of the president, the vice-president, the secretaries of state and defense, and the director of Central Intelligence. The NSC, depending on the president's preference, meets regularly to discuss foreign policy decisions.

*Nguyen Van Linh:* Linh, selected in December 1986, is the general secretary of the Communist party of the Socialist Republic Vietnam. Linh has already implemented widespread domestic economic reforms and announced plans to repair Vietnam's shattered international reputation. He surprised his domestic critics by admitting that he was the secret author of a frequent unsigned daily newspaper column entitled "Things That Must Be Done Immediately."

*The NSC staff:* Do not confuse the NSC staff with the members of the National Security Council. The NSC staff is an entity within the White

House consisting of over 70 full-time staffers, with many more support personnel. These staffers are often drawn from other Executive Branch departments, the military and the CIA. They report directly to the Assistant to the President for National Security Affairs, also known as the President's National Security Advisor.

*The Paris Peace Accords:* This agreement, signed on January 27, 1973, by the United States, North Vietnam, South Vietnam, and the Viet Cong, set forth a schedule for the withdrawal of U.S. forces from South Vietnam and the terms for the peaceful creation of a coalition government in South Vietnam. All the signatories broke the terms of this accord. Hanoi was in total control of all of Vietnam by May 1975.

*Phnom Penh:* The capitol city of Kampuchea.

*The Vessey Initiative:* In April 1987, President Reagan appointed retired army general John W. Vessey, a former chairman of the Joint Chiefs of Staff, to be a special envoy to Vietnam on the POW/MIA issue. As a result of the Vessey talks, held in Hanoi in August 1987, Washington authorized some token, private humanitarian aid for Vietnamese amputee victims of the war. Hanoi, by the terms of this agreement, pledged to act in a commensurate fashion to resolve the POW/MIA issue.

*Vientiane:* The capital city of Laos.

# BIBLIOGRAPHY

## BOOKS

*China's Hostility to Vietnam*. World Peace Council, 1979.

Herring, George. *America's Longest War*. New York: Wiley, 1979.

Kattenburg, Paul. *The Vietnam Trauma in American Foreign Policy, 1945–75*. New Brunswick: Transaction Books, 1980.

Kenny, Henry. *The American Role in Vietnam and East Asia*. New York: Praeger, 1984.

Kim, Shee Poon. *The ASEAN States' Relations with the Socialist Republic of Vietnam*. Singapore: Chopmen, 1980.

Nair, K. K. *ASEAN-Indochina Relations since 1975: The Politics of Accommodation*. London, Singapore, New York: The Strategic and Defence Studies Centre, 1984.

Nguyen, Tien Hung. *The Palace File*. New York: Harper & Row, 1986.

Patti, Archimides. *Why Vietnam?* Berkeley, Los Angeles: University of California Press, 1980.

Pike, Douglas. *Vietnam and the Soviet Union*. London: Westview Press, 1987.

Poole, Peter. *Eight Presidents and Indochina*. Huntington, N.Y.: Krieger, 1978.

*Soviet Military Power*. Washington, D.C.: U.S. Department of Defense, 1987.

## ARTICLES

Bach, William. "A Chance in Cambodia." *Foreign Policy*, Spring 1986, 75–95.

Boyd, Gerald M. "Reagan Affirms Basis for Hanoi Ties." *New York Times,* 7 June 1985.

Branigan, William. "Soviets Seek Influence in Asia-Pacific Region." *Washington Post,* 8 August 1986.

———— "ASEAN Leaders to Voice Complaints to Reagan." *Washington Post,* 25 April 1986.

———— "Haig Pledges to Shore Up Asian Allies." *Washington Post,* 19 June 1981, A1.

Buszynski, Lesek. "Vietnam's ASEAN Diplomacy: Recent Moves." *World Today,* March 1983, 98.

Chanda, Nayan. "Changing the Indochina Balance." *Far Eastern Economic Review,* 29 December 1978, 14–15.

———— "Mochtar Takes a Hand." *Far Eastern Economic Review,* 13 June 1985, 32.

Choudhury, G. W. "ASEAN and the Communist World." *Asia Pacific Community,* Summer 1981, 34.

Christian, S. "Reagan Affirms Support for Thailand." *New York Times,* 9 July 1985, A3.

Colbert, Evelyn. "United States Policy in Southeast Asia." *Current History,* April 1987, 146.

Cropsey, Seth. "Moscow in the Pacific." *National Review,* 5 June 1987, 28–30.

Crossette, Barbara. "Vietnam, Seeking Capital, Eases Rules." *New York Times,* 3 August 1987, D6.

Davies, Derek. "Carter's Neglect; Moscow's Victory." *Far Eastern Economic Review,* 2 February 1979, 16–21.

———— "The Region." *Far Eastern Economic Review Asia Yearbook,* 1982.

———— "The Region: Khmer Lodestone." *Far Eastern Economic Review Asia Yearbook,* 1981, 8–17.

Deming, Angus, Frank Gibnet, Jr., and Mark Starr. "MIA's: A Surprise from Hanoi." *Newsweek,* 22 July 1985, 34.

———— "The Rambo Syndrome." *Newsweek,* 20 January 1986, 27.

Duiker, William. "Vietnam Moves Toward Pragmatism." *Current History,* April 1987, 148.

George, T. J. S. "Vietnam: Time to Change Course." *World Press Review,* February 1987, 29.

Gordon, Bernard. "The Third Indochina Conflict." *Foreign Affairs,* Fall 1986, 66–85.

Greeley, Brendan M., Jr. "Soviets Extend Air, Sea Power with Buildup at Cam Ranh Bay." *Aviation Week,* 2 March 1987, 76–77.

Horn, Robert. "Soviet Policy in East Asia." *Current History,* October 1987, 321–40.

Huy, Nguyen Ngoc. "The Soviet-Vietnamese Alliance in Historical Perspective." *Global Affairs,* Fall 1986, 69–86.

Kaiser, Robert G. "Kennedy Calls for Indochina Peace Moves." *Washington Post,* 3 April 1979.

Kaylor, Robert. "Dominoes That Did Not Fall." *U.S. News & World Report,* 22 April 1985, 39.

———. "A Decade after Saigon's Fall." *U.S. News & World Report,* 21 January 1985, 45.

———. "Vietnam: Firmly on Course but Losing the Peace." *U.S. News & World Report,* 30 June 1986, 30.

———. "As Trouble Mounts for Communist Vietnam." *U.S. News & World Report,* 14 January 1984, 25–27.

Keleman, Paul. "Soviet Strategy in Southeast Asia: The Vietnam Factor." *Asian Survey,* March 1984, 335–48.

Kendall, Harry. "Vietnam Perceptions of the Soviet Prescence." *Asian Survey,* September 1983, 1052–61.

Koh, Tommy T. B. "Southeast Asia; Ten Years after the Vietnam War." *USA Today,* November 1985, 22.

Lee, Gary. "Gorbachev Makes Overture to Asia." *Washington Post,* 5 August 1986, A16.

Lescaze, Lee. "Chinese Invasion Seen Enhancing Peking Prestige in Southeast Asia." *Washington Post,* 8 March 1979, A17.

Luce, Don. "The Boat People." *Progressive,* September 1979, 27–29.

McDonald, Hamish. "The Cam Ranh Bugbear." *Far Eastern Economic Review,* 18 June 1987, 34.

Morris, Stephen. "Vietnam's Vietnam." *Atlantic Monthly,* January 1985, 71–82.

Musil, Robert. "Manipulating the MIA's." *Nation,* 9 October 1976, 331–34.

Nations, Richard. "Great Leap Sideways." *Far Eastern Economic Review,* 30 May 1985, 15–16.

———. "Hanoi's MIA Card." *Far Eastern Economic Review,* 18 July 1985, 15–16.

———. "The Missing Link." *Far Eastern Economic Review,* 19 November 1982, 10–11.

Oberdorfer, D., and Branigan, William. "Haig Warns Hanoi on Ties." *Washington Post,* 21 June 1981.

Oberdorfer, Don. "Asians Reject Soviet Ship Visits." *Washington Post,* 19 September 1979.

———. "Asia's Dominoes Didn't Fall after Vietnam, They Got Rich Instead." *Washington Post,* 29 July 1984, C1.

———. "11 Nations on Pacific Rim Forge New Ties." *Washington Post,* 14 July 1984, A12.

Pike, Douglas. "American-Vietnam Relations." *Parameters,* Autumn 1984, 21–31.

——— "Vietnam in 1977: More of the Same." *Asian Survey,* January 1978, 68–75.

——— "The U.S.S.R. and Vietnam: Into the Swamp." *Asian Survey,* December 1979, 1159–70.

——— "Vietnam in 1981: Biting the Bullet." *Asian Survey,* January 1982, 69–77.

——— "Vietnam and the Regional Security of Southeast Asia." *Global Affairs,* Winter 1987, 101–12.

Porter, Gareth. " 'Healing the Wounds of War'; Justice Not Charity for Vietnam." *Christian Century,* 2 March 1977, 192–94.

——— "China in Southeast Asia." *Current History,* April 1987, 249.

"President's Address before ASEAN Ministers Meeting, May 1, 1986." Department of State Bulletin, July 1986.

Rowny, Edward. "Arms Control: The East Asian and Pacific Focus." Department of State Bulletin, March 1987, 37–39.

Schneider, Eberhard. "Soviet Vietnam Policy, 1975–1976." *Aussenpolitik* (first quarter 1977): 15-34.

Sethi, Patricia J. "The Door Is Open." *Newsweek,* 14 May 1984, 39.

Shaplen, Robert. "Return to Vietnam, Part One." *New Yorker,* 22 April 1985, 104–25.

Tasker, Rodney. "Stealing the Thunder." *Far Eastern Economic Review,* 18 July 1985, 14–15.

Terzani, Tiziano. "Vietnam in Trouble." *World Press Review,* November 1981, 28–30.

Tuan, Nguyen Anh. "Impact of U.S. Policy in Southeast Asia in Retrospect." *Global Affairs,* Winter 1987, 113–29.

"Vietnam under Two Regimes." Department of State Bulletin, September 1985, 51–56.

"Vietnam's Future Policies and Role in Southeast Asia." U.S. Senate Committee on Foreign Relations Report, 1982, 72.

Weatherbee, Donald E. "U.S. Policy and the Two Southeast Asias." *Asian Survey,* April 1978, 408–21.

Weinstein, Franklin B. "U.S.-Vietnamese Relations and the Security of Southeast Asia." *Foreign Affairs,* July 1978, 842–56.

Whitaker, Mark, Frank Gibney, Jr., and Kim Witenson. "The Lost Americans." *Newsweek,* 20 January 1986, 26–27.

Willesrud, Aasmund. "Normalization Eludes Vietnam." *World Press Review.* April 1984, 27.

Wolfowitz, Paul. "Accounting for American POWs/MIAs in Southeast Asia." Department of State Bulletin, September 1985, 56–59.

Yahuda, Michael. "China's New Outlook." *World Today,* May 1979, 180.

Young, Stephen B. "Unpopular Socialism in Vietnam." *Orbis,* Summer 1977, 227–39.

Zheenmin, Mei. "Vietnam: Occupation of Kampuchea Harmful to Economy." *Beijing Review,* 12 January 1987, 11.

# INDEX

## ABOUT THE AUTHOR

JOHN LeBOUTILLIER was elected to the U.S. House of Representatives in 1980. At the age of twenty-seven, he was the youngest member of the House. He was selected to serve on the House Foreign Affairs Committee, the International Security Subcommittee, the International Organizations and Human Rights Subcommittee, and the House Task Force on American POWs and MIAs in Southeast Asia.

In 1981 and 1982, LeBoutillier made four trips to Southeast Asia and helped to achieve a breakthrough warming of relations between Washington and the Laotian government. In 1988, he was the invited guest of the Vietnamese government for a week of talks in Hanoi. LeBoutillier wrote of this unique journey in the Sunday *New York Times Magazine*.

A magna cum laude graduate of Harvard University and a graduate of the Harvard Business School, LeBoutillier wrote the critically acclaimed *Harvard Hates America* in 1978. He coauthored a novel, *Primary,* in 1979 with James C. Humes.

LeBoutillier is the founder and president of Account for POW/MIAs, Inc., the largest nonprofit organization attempting to gather information on American prisoners of war still held against their will in Southeast Asia. He is also the president of Accuracy in Academia and the chairman of the board of the Winston Churchill Foundation.